LOCOMOTION PAPERS

The Yate to Thornbury Branch

by

Colin G. Maggs

THE OAKWOOD PRESS

British Library Cataloguing in Publication Data
A Record for this book is available from the British Library
ISBN 0 85361 585 3

Typeset by Oakwood Graphics.
Repro by Ford Graphics, Ringwood, Hants.
Printed by Inkon Printers Ltd, Yateley, Hants.

Fireman Royston Tucker watches '4F' class 0-6-0 No. 44296 being driven off the turntable at Thornbury, September 1963. *W.F. Grainger*

Title page: '16XX' class 0-6-0PT No. 1625 ready for departure with the Railway Enthusiasts' Club's 'Severn Venturer' at Thornbury on 15th April, 1956. *M.E.J. Deane*

Front cover: A class '4F' 0-6-0 is seen at Thornbury in 1964 with a train of hopper wagons. *Derek Chaplin*

Rear cover: Class '59' Co-Co No. 59203 *Vale of Pickering* stands at Tytherington Quarry with a train for Fareham on 24th August, 2000. *Author*

Published by The Oakwood Press (Usk), P.O. Box 13, Usk, Mon., NP15 1YS.
E-mail: oakwood-press@dial.pipex.com
Website: www.oakwood-press.dial.pipex.com

Contents

Chapter One	**The Construction and Opening of the Thornbury and Frampton Cotterell Branches**	5
Chapter Two	**Description of the Line**	13
Chapter Three	**Closure and Re-Opening**	67
Chapter Four	**The Passenger Train Services**	81
Chapter Five	**Goods and Mineral Traffic**	93
Chapter Six	**Locomotives and Working**	119
Chapter Seven	**Signalling, Permanent Way and Mishaps**	129
Appendix One	**Traffic at Tytherington (1941-1949)**	140
Appendix Two	**Traffic at Thornbury (1941-1954)**	141
Appendix Three	**Goods Traffic (1960s)**	142
	Acknowledgements	143
	Bibliography	143
	Index	144

Class '4F' 0-6-0 No. 44534 with a train to Yate, on Latteridge crossing, March 1964.
W.F. Grainger

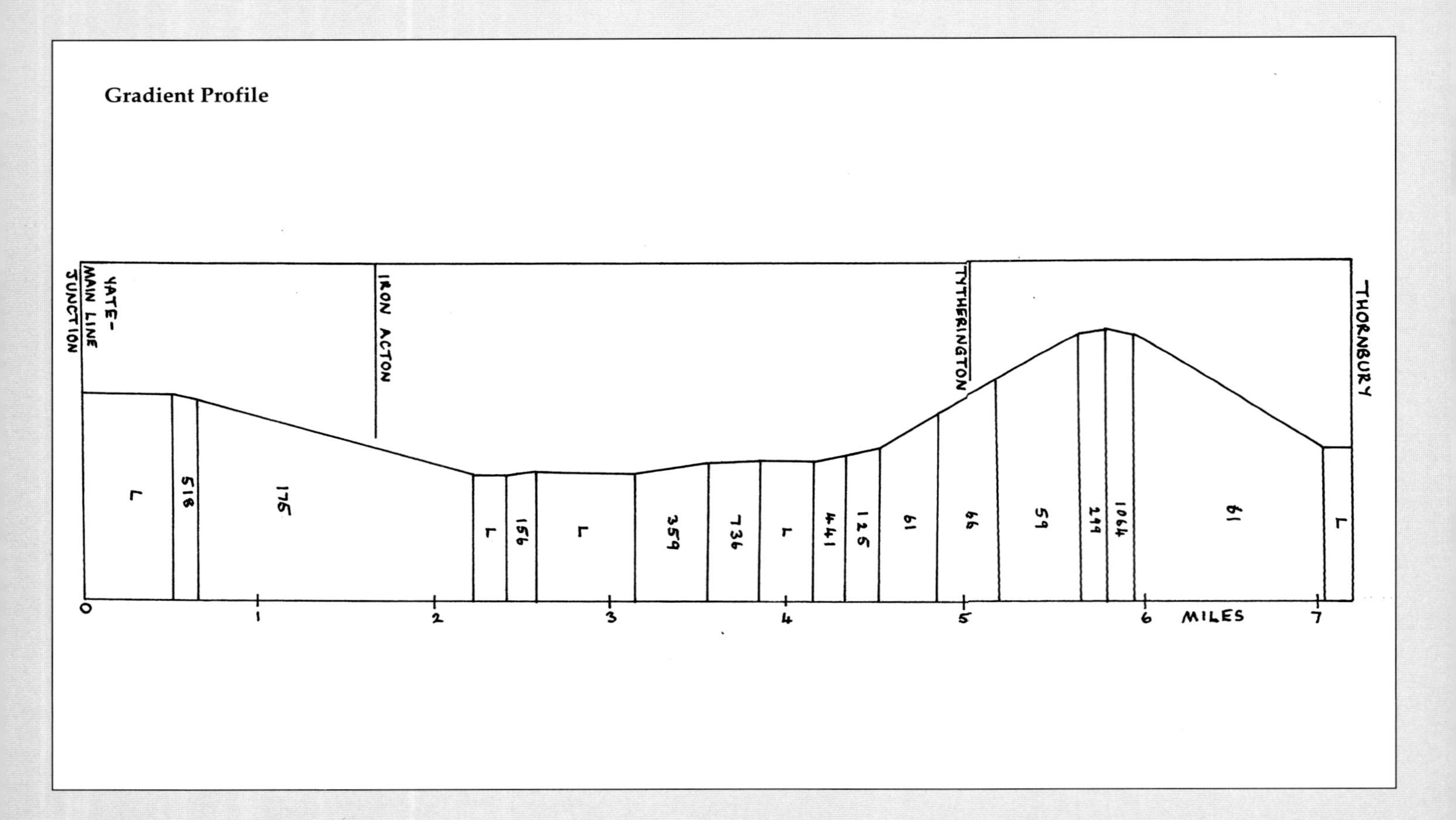

Gradient Profile

Chapter One

The Constuction and Opening of the Thornbury and Frampton Cotterell Branches

Midway between Bristol and Gloucester lies Thornbury, three miles from the River Severn and separated from it by marshy land long since drained. The town was granted borough status in the mid-13th century. Its greatest historical personality was Edward Stafford, Duke of Buckingham, who built his castle on the edge of the town, but lost his head during Henry VIII's reign. The turnpike road, later the A38, kept to the higher and better-drained ground and so passed a mile to the south-east. Until 1911 the market, specialising in livestock and cheese, was held in the wide High Street.

The Bristol & Gloucester Railway opened on 8th July, 1844 and was amalgamated with the Midland Railway (MR) in 1846. Yate and Wickwar were the nearest stations to Thornbury, both about five miles distant as the crow flies, but rather more for folk using meandering lanes. Less than two miles from Yate is Iron Acton, the name dating back to at least 1248 and derived from the tun, or township timbered with ac or oak, where iron is dug. It is interesting to learn that extra strong roofing timbers were required for local houses because the iron content made the stone roofing tiles so heavy. In 1858 the manager and lessee of the iron ore mines pressed for a railway to be built to Iron Acton. The haematite, set in vertical fissures, was worked to a depth of 360 ft, with levels at 180 ft, 240 ft and 360 ft. Workings extended about 3,000 ft from east to west.

The Yate & Thornbury Act, together with the Mangotsfield & Bath Act, both 27 & 28 Vict. cap. 164, received Royal Assent on 14th July, 1864. The authorised capital for the combined lines was set at £236,000 in shares and £78,600 in loans. John Sydney Crossley the MR's Chief Engineer, was appointed Engineer to both the Bath and Thornbury lines, his greatest achievement being the Settle & Carlisle Railway.

On 31st October, 1864 the manager and lessee of the mines at Iron Acton was said to be 'very pressing' for a 1 mile 7 chain long branch to be made to his pit at Frampton Cotterell just south of Iron Acton. On 31st January, 1865 Crossley reported that the survey for this branch was almost finished, but soon after he made this announcement, poor weather delayed its completion and the survey was not finished until May. On 21st June, 1865 Ashmead & Son, Bristol, were appointed land valuers at the usual terms of £30 per mile. This branch line running from a junction with the Thornbury line at Iron Acton to almost opposite Frampton Cotterell church, was authorised by 28 & 29 Vict. cap. 335 which received Royal Assent on 5th July, 1865, this Act covered 15 various short lines totalling 31¾ miles in connection with the MR's existing system. It was decided that both the Thornbury and Frampton Cotterell lines would be proceeded with concurrently and the former was staked out in September 1865.

In July 1866 the following tenders were received for building the line for which Crossley estimated the cost to be £59,652 0*s.* 0*d.*

Eckersley & Bayliss	£69,907	0*s.*	0*d.*
J. Firbank	£77,312	6*s.*	8*d.*
Benton & Woodiwiss	£81,486	6*s.*	8*d.*

MIDLAND RAILWAY.

Regulations for Working the Yate and Thornbury Branch.

1.—No more than one Engine must ever be allowed to be on the Branch at one time, except in the case of an Engine that has entered the Branch becoming disabled and requiring assistance, when the Guard of the Train, the Engine of which has become disabled, must instruct the Driver to keep the Engine stationary until his return, and then make the best of his way to the Signalman on duty at the Yate Station, and inform him of the circumstance; and the Signalman will, on receipt of such information, allow a second Engine to enter the Branch to the assistance of the first. The second Engine must be accompanied by the Guard of the disabled Train, who must explain to the Driver where, and under what circumstances the disabled Train is situated.

2.—The Guard of the disabled Train will be held responsible for the safe and proper working of the Branch until both Engines have left it, and it is again clear.

3.—In the case of an Engine without a Guard becoming disabled on the Branch, the Fireman must perform the duties prescribed for the Guard.

4.—All Points and Stop-blocks of Sidings connected with the Main Line must be kept securely locked, except when required to be used for the purpose of shunting vehicles with an Engine.

5.—The Station-master at the Yate Station is held responsible for taking care that these Regulations are strictly carried out.

6.—If any breach of these Regulations should occur, it must be immediately reported to the Superintendent of the Line at Derby.

JAMES ALLPORT,
General Manager.

Derby, July, 1868.

Regulations for working the Yate and Thornbury branch, July 1868. The line was not opened to Frampton until May 1869 and not to Thornbury until 2nd September, 1872!

Eckersley's tender was accepted on 31st July, 1866. Landowners were not anxious to sell their property to the railway and it was necessary to take compulsory possession, so it was not possible to hand the route from Yate to Iron Acton to the contractor until 31st May, 1867. Work started on three cuttings and the foundation of the bridge across the River Frome on the Frampton branch on 30th June. Progress was also made with fencing, but owing to the non-possession of land, works were almost brought to a stand in August 1867.

The land between Iron Acton and Frampton Cotterell was eventually handed to Eckersley & Bayliss on 18th December, 1867. By that date five of the eight bridges between Yate and Frampton were almost complete. Work certainly proceeded apace for on 30th March, 1868 Crossley reported that except for 400 yards, all the permanent way had been laid between Yate and Frampton Cotterell, assuring the Bath & Thornbury Construction Committee that 'All will be ready for the mines before they are ready for traffic'. The *Bristol Observer* of 21st March, 1868 reported: 'During the whole of Sunday March 15th, 134 men and 13 horses were employed on the railway between Iron Acton and Frampton Cotterell'. The 2 miles 72 chains of line to Frampton, together with the transfer siding at Yate was opened in May 1868, the exact date not being recorded. The *Bath Chronicle* of 2nd December, 1869 reported:

> A valuable seam of ironstone, second to none in the kingdom for richness, is now being developed at Frampton Cotterell, from where there is a branch line to the Yate station of the Midland Railway. The mine will yield a vast quantity of haematite.

Regarding the Iron Acton to Thornbury section, on 2nd February, 1869 Crossley reported to the MR's Construction Committee the desirability of replacing the open cutting at the summit, approached on both sides by a gradient of 1 in 60, with two tunnels. Following the committee's assent, on 6th July, 1869 he reported that he had arranged with Eckersley & Bayliss to cut the tunnels at £15 a yard. Meanwhile on 6th April, 1869 Crossley reported that the line at Tytherington village was complete. The line between Iron Acton and Tytherington was finished on 3rd August, 1869, but it was thought that until the line to Thornbury was ready, it would be doubtful if working would be economic. On 29th May, 1869 the Construction Committee queried the site of Iron Acton station, but Crossley observed that its position was determined by the junction with the Frampton branch.

In 1869, John Allen McDonald, born at Bristol in 1847, was appointed engineer to Eckersley & Bayliss and so brought into contact with Crossley. In July 1890 McDonald was appointed Chief Engineer to the MR, his last and greatest work being the construction of Heysham harbour in conjunction with G.N. Abernethy.

On 4th April, 1870 Crossley reported that the 224 yds-long tunnel was complete and the 167 yds-long Grovesend tunnel (below what was later to be the A38) was half cut; by 30th May, 1870 only three small bridges and 20 yards of tunnel awaited completion. On 31st August the formation was complete from Iron Acton to Grovesend tunnel. Work then seems to have become rather slower, for on 28th February, 1871, Crossley reported that two bridges still had to be built and a cutting excavated, work on the line being increased by slips brought down by frost. A letter of 1st June stated that the partnership between Eckersley & Bayliss had been dissolved and that the contract would be completed by Bayliss alone, who, incidentally, was also responsible for building the northern half of the Settle & Carlisle Railway.

In June 1871 the following tenders were received:

	Crossley	*S. Robertson*	*E. Niblett*	*W. Eassie*	*G. Peters*	*J. Roach*	*Ambrose*
Thornbury station building	600	558	405		429		548
Turntable foundation	235	248	192	1,000	222		204
Grovesend station*	380	386	368		410		
Tytherington	380	376	368		409		
Frampton Cotterell station*	380	376	368	975	406		
Iron Acton Cottage	160	155	125		146	178	378
Acton Court Cottage (Latteridge)	160	155	125		146	178	
	2,295	2,254	1,951	1,975	2,168	356	1,130

That of Edwin Niblett, Gloucester, was accepted.

On 6th February, 1872 further tenders were considered:

	Station Master's House Tytherington			*Station Master's House Thornbury*			*Goods Warehouse Thornbury*		
	£	*s.*	*d.*	*£*	*s.*	*d.*	*£*	*s.*	*d.*
Crossley's estimate	300	0	0	300	0	0	695	0	0
G. Peters	357	6	9	357	6	9	826	9	0
Alfred Ridout	320	0	0	320	0	0	715	0	0
Samuel Robertson	288	10	0	288	10	0	664	13	0
Edwin Niblett	299	1	4	299	1	4	688	16	5

Robertson's tender was accepted.

Track laying was completed by 5th March, 1872 and on this date, at Thornbury, the foundation was awaiting the turntable, while the station buildings were ready for roofing; the platform was finished, as was the temporary booking office. It was anticipated that the buildings at Tytherington station would be completed in two weeks; that at Iron Acton merely required a coat of paint; the level crossing cottage at Latteridge only needed its roof, while at Iron Acton, its counterpart was roofed and the station master's house built up to the ground floor window sills. On 19th March, 1872 it was decided to alter the sidings at Yate and provide a locomotive turntable there. On 30th April, 1872 the Works & Traffic Committee agreed that Thornbury station should be fitted with gas lighting at a cost of £70 13*s*. 0*d*. The level crossing lodge at Iron Acton was adapted and enlarged for the station master at a cost of £90.

Lt Col C.S. Hutchinson inspected the line in mid-August 1872 and reported to the Board of Trade:

* Not built.

19th August, 1872

Sir,

I have the honour to report for the information of the Board of Trade, in compliance with the instructions contained in your Minute of 8th Inst., that I have inspected the Midland Railway Company's new branch line from Yate to Thornbury.

This line is 7 miles 37 chains in length and is single throughout except at its junction with the main line from Gloucester to Bristol at Yate, and at its terminus at Thornbury, where there are sidings.

The Gauge is 4 ft 8½ in. and there is an interval of 6 ft between the lines where there is more than one. Land has been purchased and some of the works constructed with a view to the line being doubled hereafter.

In addition to the station at Thornbury there are also stations and without sidings [*sic*] at Iron Acton (where a mineral branch joins the main line) and at Tytherington.

The width of the line at formation level is 15 ft in Cuttings and 19 ft on Embankments.

The rails are double headed in 20 ft lengths weighing 80 lbs per yd fished at the joints. They are secured by inside keys to chairs of cast iron weighing 34 lbs each. The chairs are secured to the Sleepers by two Iron Spikes in each. The sleepers are of Baltic timber, rectangular in Section measuring 9 ft x 10 in. x 5 in., 2 ft from centre to centre at the joints and 3 ft intermediately. The ballast is of broken stone stated to be 1 ft deep below the under surface of the sleepers.

Engine turntables have been provided at Yate and Thornbury. The fencing consists for the most part of post and rail with some portions of stone walling.

There are in all 10 bridges, viaducts and aqueducts over and under the line. Seven of these are over bridges, 6 constructed entirely of masonry the largest span being 31 ft on the skew, and 1 a timber footbridge with a span of 48 ft. One is an iron aqueduct carrying a stream over the line; and the remaining 10 are under bridges or viaducts constructed entirely of masonry, or of masonry abutments with cast iron and wrot. iron girders, the largest span being 28 ft.

These bridges etc. appear to be all substantially Constructed [*sic*] and to be standing well. In the case of the under bridges with wrot. iron girders the deflections under a rolling stock load were, owing to the comparative small depth of the webs, somewhat greater than usual.

There are two tunnels on the line 220 and 166 yards in length respectively, partially lined.

There are also two authorized, public road level crossings provided with lodges and proper gates.

The steepest gradient on the line has an inclination of 1 in 59 and the sharpest curve a radius of 16 chains.

There have been some unauthorized vertical deviations from the parliamentary section, but these do not appear to have been objected to by the landowners and do not affect the safety of the public in the working of the traffic.

I observed the following deficiencies in the course of my inspection.

1. Clocks and names are not yet provided at the stations.
2. Some gaps in the fencing require making good.
3. The level crossing gates must be prevented from opening outwards.
4. The view of the Up distant at Yate and of the down distant Signal at Iron Acton requires improving. Clocks are required in the junction Cabins. The mineral branch at Iron Acton junction requires providing with an interlocked safety siding. At Yate Junction a crossover road is to come out and the up arrival signal to be repeated into the cabin.
5. A projecting point of rock in one of the tunnels requires removal.
6. The ballasting is not in all cases completed.
7. Holding down bolts, wedges, and ballast are required on the under bridges.

These matters are to be at once attended to and upon condition that their completion is notified to the Board of Trade and that an inspection shall take place at some future time, the opening of the line for passenger traffic might I submit have been sanctioned had a satisfactory undertaking as to the mode of working the traffic been received; but pending its receipt I have to report that by reason of the incompleteness of the works the line from Yate to Thornbury cannot be opened for passenger traffic without danger to the public using the same.

I have &c

C.S. Hutchinson

Lieut Col RE

The MR gave the necessary undertaking and the line was permitted to be opened to public traffic.

Opening to Thornbury

On Saturday 31st August, 1872 a MR Director, John Mercer of Clifton; E.M. Needham, general superintendent; J.A. Warwick, superintendent of telegraphs; Mr Winn, district engineer and other officials, left Bristol by train at 8.30 am and 'proceeded over the line for the purpose of seeing that all was made ready for traffic; depositing the furniture, staff &c at the stations between Yate and Thornbury' - *Bristol Times & Mirror* 3rd September, 1872.

The first public train ran from Bristol to Thornbury on 2nd September, 1872 and set down about 100 passengers at Thornbury, while 53 booked on the first train from Thornbury to Bristol. J.C. Gwynn, solicitor and Mayor of Thornbury, left Bristol by the first train and was welcomed to his town by a brass band. On alighting from the train, the *Bristol Times & Mirror* reported: 'He was handed into a carriage and drawn in triumph by the inhabitants to the Swan Hotel where his worship received the congratulations of some of the principal inhabitants of the town'. The *Bristol Mercury* observed that MR Directors and leading officials were not at the opening and seemed not to like the branch and commented that if they had attended, a celebratory luncheon would have been held. The *Bristol Times & Mirror* also had reservations. After pointing out that hitherto passengers to Thornbury had to travel on the Bristol & South Wales Union Railway from Bristol to Patchway and then catch a bus, in continued: '. . . unless time is an object, it is very probable that this will continue to be a favourite route, for it is not only a pleasanter, but cheaper journey'. The MR fare for Bristol to Thornbury was 1*s*. 5½*d*. third class, 2*s*. 4*d*. second and 4*s*. 0*d*. first class return, whereas the rail fares from Bristol to Patchway were only 6*d*., 9*d*. and 1*s*. 3*d*. respectively, with a horse bus return fare of 8*d*. outside and 10*d*. inside and, furthermore, travelling by bus '. . . he would have thrown in one of the most charming drives to be found in this part of the country; for it will be acknowledged that the woodland and Severn scenery from Almondsbury to Thornbury is of the most picturesque kind'.

Despite the lack of enthusiasm displayed by both the Directors and the *Times & Mirror*, Thornbury was *en fete*. The *Times & Mirror* grew more enthusiastic later in its report. 'At the railway station scarcely standing room could be obtained, so great was the crush of people, several thousands of persons having assembled there to await the arrival of the first train from Bristol'. Most shops closed at 11.30 am; streets were decorated with flags and arches; while bells rang from the parish church. At 1.30 pm 725 schoolchildren from the Church of England, Dissenting and Union schools, accompanied by their teachers and the Alveston band, travelled in an 18-coach train to Yate at 4*d*. return per head, the cost being defrayed by public subscription. When they arrived back at Thornbury, the children were let out for a run near the station in fields lent by Mr R. Scarlett, solicitor. Here they sat down to a substantial tea, the cake provided by Mr Vowles, the Thornbury baker.

> Many of the residents in Thornbury illuminated their dwellings at night, gas stars and other brilliant devices being apparent on every hand; while to add to the other attractions, Mr Penley, pyrotechnist, of Wotton-under-Edge, made a display of fireworks. The last train that left Thornbury for Yate was densely crowded by persons, who went to the junction and back again for the novelty of the ride by rail, and numbers of rustics showed by their exclamations that they had not until yesterday seen a locomotive. A little inconvenience was experienced on account of the rush of passengers, but Mr Brant, the station master, and his assistants, proved equal to the emergency, and the arrangements on a less exacting occasion may be expected to work smoothly. Simply for an excursion, a trip along the new route would repay the traveller, as in the locality of Tytherington the scenery is very bold and romantic, and similar in character to that at the Peak in Derbyshire, which is perhaps unequalled in England (*Western Daily Press*, 3rd September, 1872).

YATE, FRAMPTON, AND THORNBURY.

Miles.	STATIONS.	WEEK DAYS. 58 Goods, &c.	59 Passenger	60	61 Passenger
		a. m.	a. m.		p. m.
..	YATE ....dep.	8 50	9 40	..	5 25
..	Iron Acton Junc....	8 55	..	..	..
..	Frampton Cottrel	9 2	..	..	..
2	Iron Acton	..	9 4[illegible]	..	5 34
5¼	Tytherington	..	10 1	..	5 46
7½	THORNBURY arr.	..	10 10	..	5 55

Miles.	STATIONS.	WEEK DAYS. 62 Passenger	63 Goods, &c.	64	65 Passenger
		a. m.	a. m.		p. m.
..	THORNBURY dep.	8 10	..	..	4 35
2¼	Tytherington	8 19	..	..	4 44
5½	Iron Acton	8 31	..	..	4 55
..	Frampton Cottrel	..	9 18	..	..
..	Iron Acton Junc....	..	9 26	..	..
7½	YATE.........arr.	8 40	9 30	..	5 2

Working timetable July 1872.

Westerleigh sidings looking in the up direction, 21st April, 1960. The main Bristol to Gloucester line is on the right. The siding on the far left is for sole use of repairers Marcroft Wagons Ltd, its buildings being adjacent. *Author*

Yate South Junction signal box 18th February, 1961. The ex-LMS double line is to and from Bristol; the branch on the left leads to Westerleigh West Junction and that on the right from Westerleigh West Junction, the latter having crossed the ex-LMS line by a bridge about half a mile to the south. *D. Payne*

Chapter Two

Description of the Line

To put Yate station into context it should be explained that 2½ miles south was the Midland Railway's Westerleigh marshalling yard with 13 up and 12 down roads opened 1900-1 to ease congestion at Bath and Bristol. Due to a reduction in rail freight, the yard closed on 19th January, 1965. Part of the site was re-developed 20 years later as Avon County Council's Westerleigh Refuse Terminal, from where, until 30th March, 2001, containers were sent to Calvert, Buckinghamshire. On 1st March, 1991 another section of the site was opened as a Murco Petroleum oil distribution depot. Another part of the site is used as an engineer's training school and secure compound for the storage of on-track maintenance machines.

Midway between the marshalling yard and Yate station, the Great Western Railway's (GWR) Wootton Bassett to Filton line, opened in 1903, crossed the MR by a three-arch stone bridge. Immediately to the east was the triangular Westerleigh Junction with signal boxes at the northern, western and eastern apexes. Beyond Westerleigh North Junction the up and down roads bifurcated, the up line (towards Birmingham) crossing the MR by means of a flying junction and joining it at Yate South Junction signal box. The eastern side of the triangle between Westerleigh North Junction and East Junction has had quite an eventful history. Taken out of use on 18th December, 1916 it was reinstated 18th February, 1918; taken out of use again on 10th July, 1927 and then re-opened for wartime traffic on 16th August, 1942. It finally closed on 4th January, 1950, the track not being lifted until *circa* 1965. The Queen and Prince Philip were in the Royal train stabled overnight on this spur *circa* 1953. It was ganger Sid Nelson's duty to visit the site and ensure all the facilities were functioning correctly. When under one coach, the flush was pulled! Today, between Westerleigh Junction(formerly Westerleigh West Junction), and the Tytherington branch junction at Yate Middle, the up line is signalled for reversible working so that a train from Tytherington does not gain the down road until it reaches Westerleigh Junction.

Yate station (119 miles 65 chains from Derby), was of Brunel design and planned either by him or his staff as he was Engineer to the Bristol & Gloucester Railway. The station, similar to Pangbourne and Twyford on the GWR, was a pleasing design executed in brick, relieved with stone, the main offices were situated on the down platform, while opposite was a delightful waiting shelter in pavilion style. Both buildings had flat canopies to protect passengers from the weather. As these awnings had no slope to enable rain water to drain off, they were weather-proofed with a sheet of lead fixed to the canopy with flat-sided, round-topped battens over which the lead was rolled. This resulted, in a decorative, shining, ribbed surface. The main building had Tudor-style chimneys, doors and windows and a steep-gabled roof. The platforms were extended by Samuel Robertson in 1865. Rather unusually, no bay platform was provided, so branch passenger trains had to use the main line platforms. Mail bag apparatus was installed in 1898 but was out of use by 1941. In the 1950s oil-lamps illuminated the goods yard, passenger platform and weighbridge house,

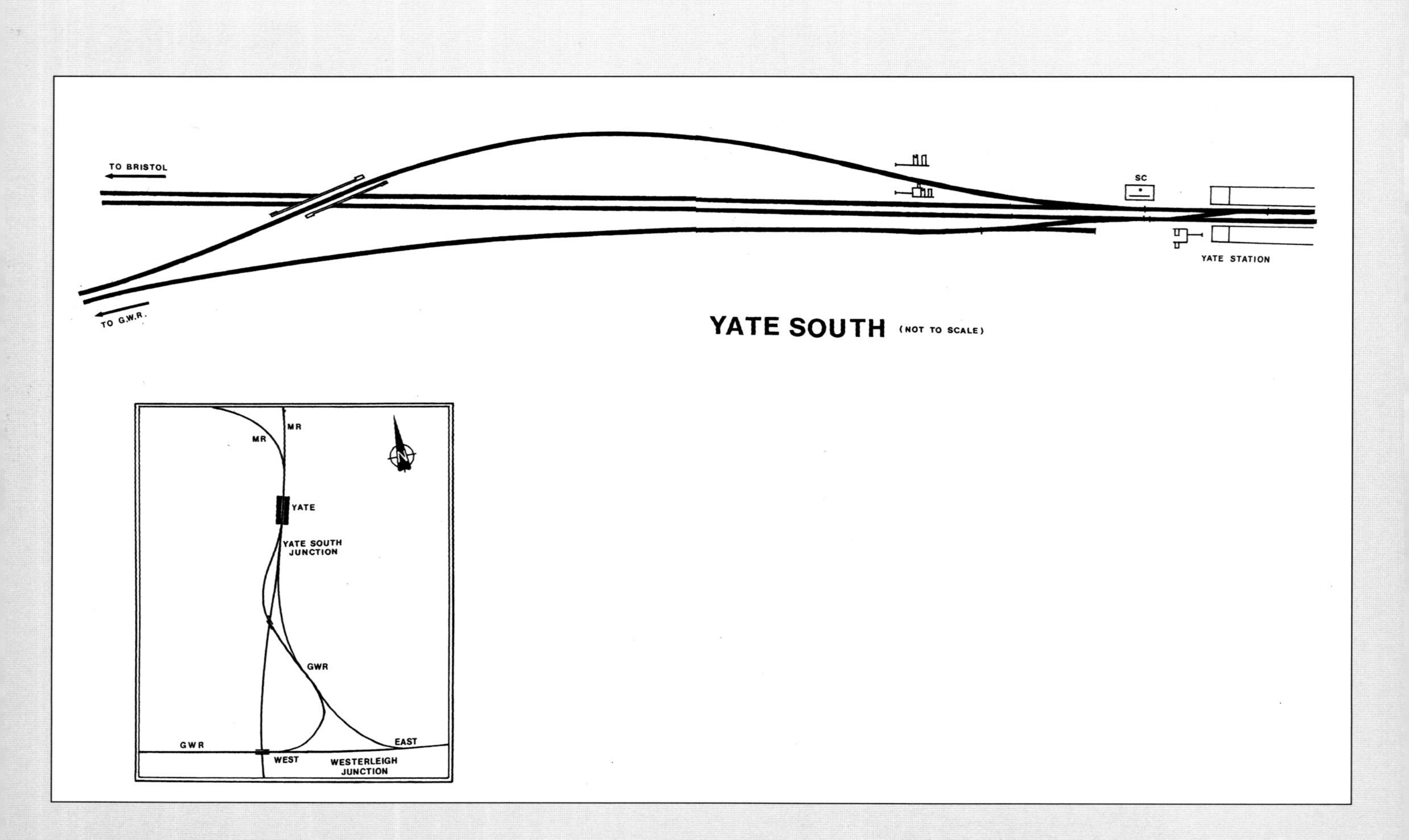
TO BRISTOL
TO G.W.R.
SC
YATE STATION
YATE SOUTH (NOT TO SCALE)
MR
MR
YATE
YATE SOUTH JUNCTION
GWR
GWR
EAST
WEST
WESTERLEIGH JUNCTION

BR Standard class '5' 4-6-0 No. 73021 stands at Yate South Junction home signal waiting for a train from Westerleigh West Junction to pass. Yate station is in the distance, 17th August, 1963. *W.F. Grainger*

Class '4F' 0-6-0 No. 44534 of 82E (Bristol, Barrow Road), with a train for Thornbury, in October 1963 waits at Yate South Junction signal box for an up train from Westerleigh West Junction which will pass to the right of the right-hand platelayers' hut. *W.F. Grainger*

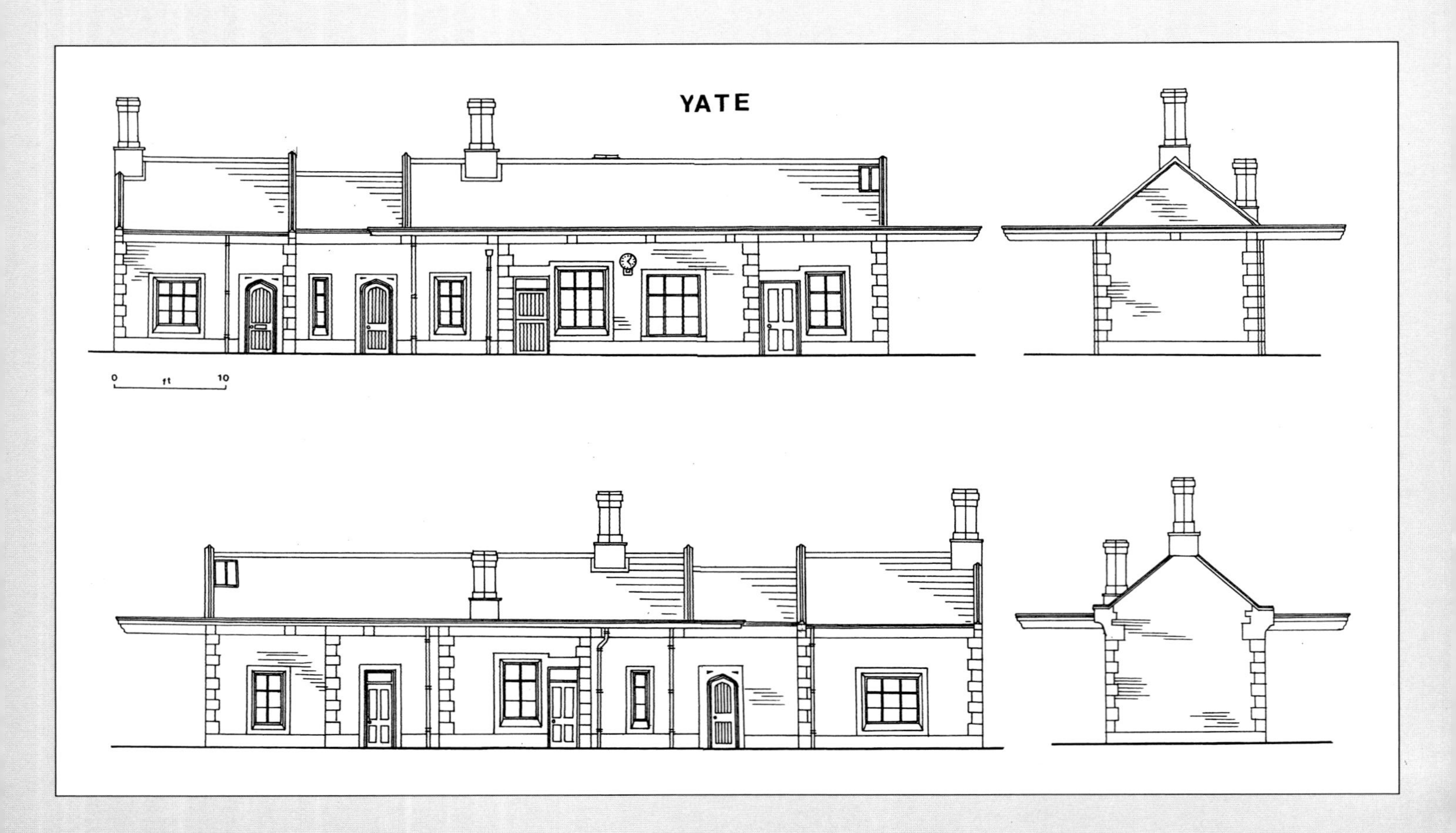
YATE
0
ft
10

YATE

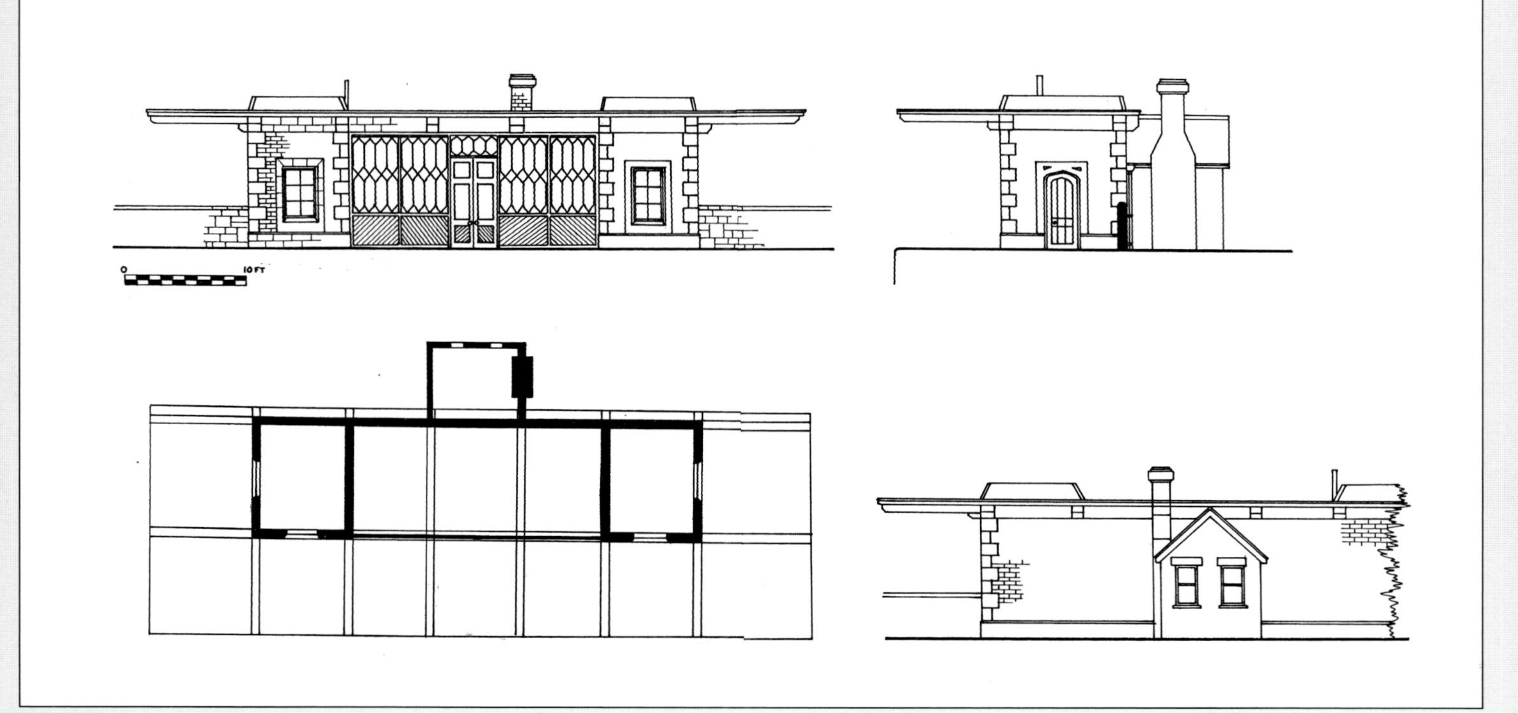

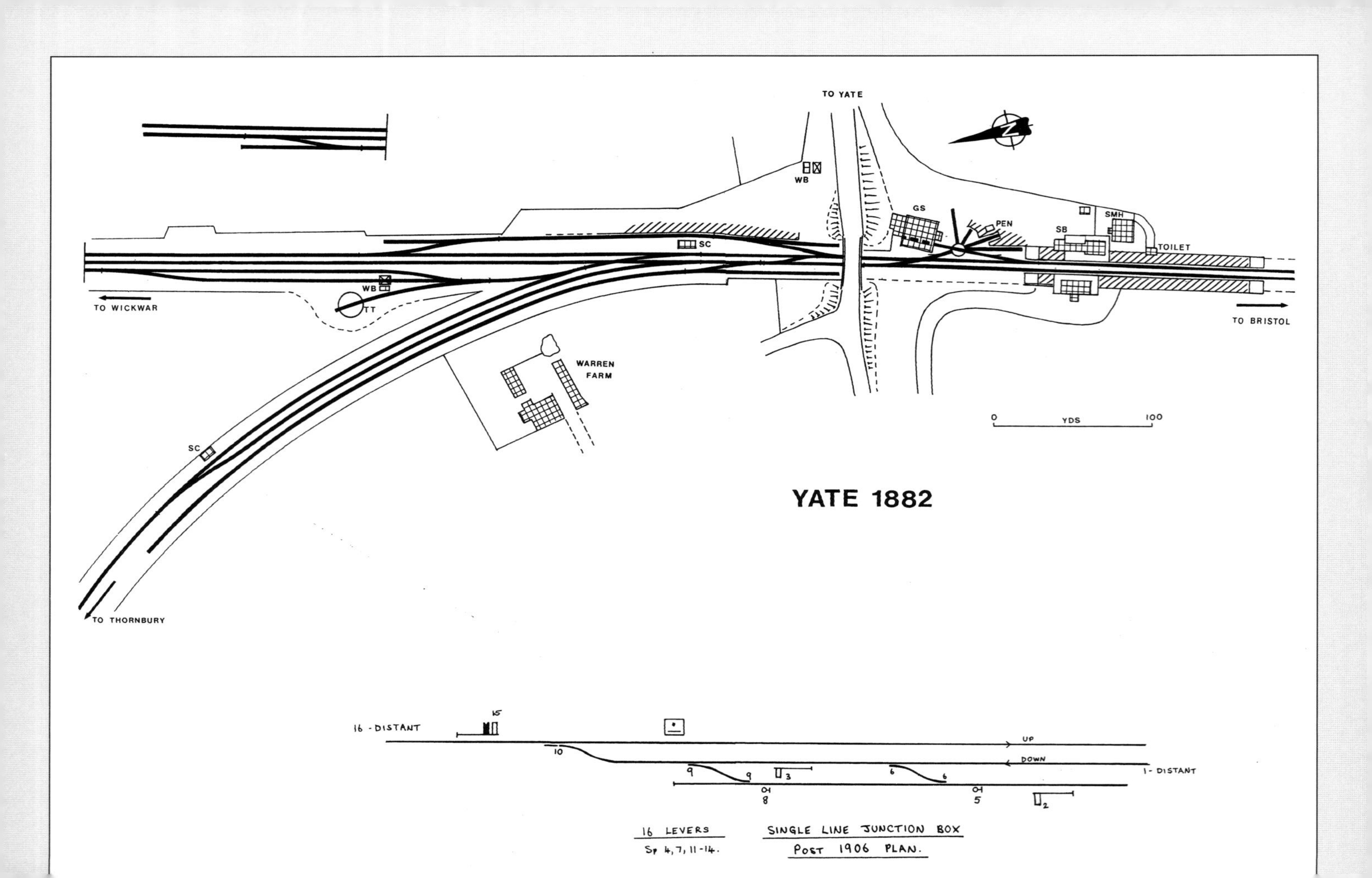
YATE 1882
TO YATE
TO WICKWAR
TO BRISTOL
TO THORNBURY
WB
GS
PEN
SB
SMH
TOILET
SC
TT
WARREN FARM
0
YDS
100
16 - DISTANT
15
10
UP
DOWN
1 - DISTANT
9
3
6
8
5
2
16 LEVERS
Sp 4, 7, 11-14.
SINGLE LINE JUNCTION BOX
POST 1906 PLAN.

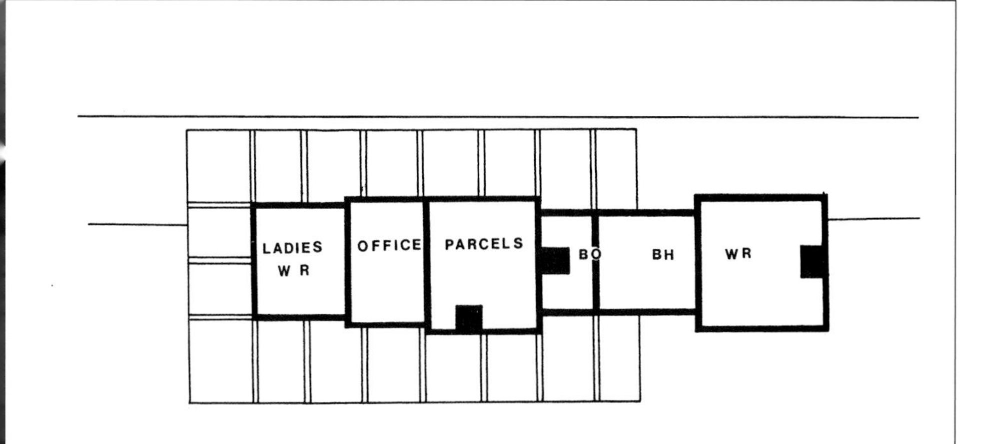
LADIES
W R
OFFICE
PARCELS
BO
BH
WR

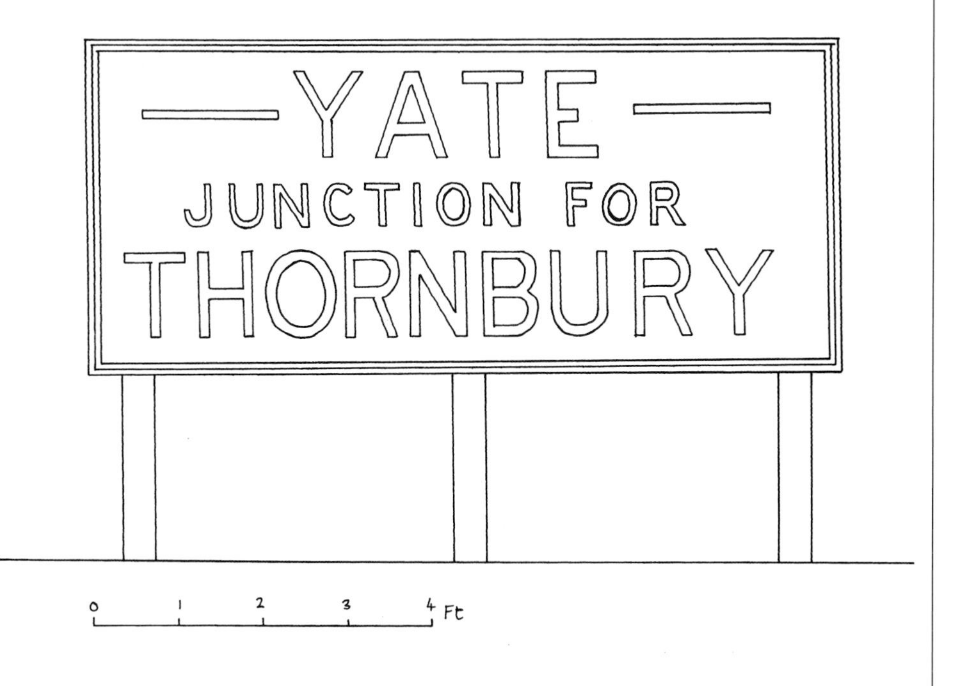
YATE
JUNCTION FOR
THORNBURY
0 1 2 3 4 Ft

A 5-coach down train arrives at Yate *c.*1905 headed by a class '1P' 0-4-4T. The station master's house is on the far right. *M.J. Tozer Collection*

The building on Yate down platform, *c.*1910. *Author's Collection*

while electric lighting was utilised in the goods shed, mess room, foreman's cabin, station offices and the two signal boxes.

The station closed to passengers on 4th January, 1965 and to goods on 20th June, 1966. The stone station house and the brick-built goods shed, relieved with Bath stone, still stand, the latter situated in a very cramped position between the down platform and a road overbridge. To make the utmost use of the confined space, short sidings radiated from a wagon turntable which had flush timber decking, though the surrounding ground was not raised to this level. Wagons were moved on and off the turntable and sidings by a pinch bar. A trap point prevented any vehicle from fouling the main line. North of the overbridge were more sidings.

Joseph Hall was station master at the end of the 19th century and the beginning of the 20th. As the station house was small and his family large, all his sons slept in one bed lying head to toe. One son later ran a coal business at Yate and this was taken over by the Fishponds Coal Co. *circa* 1940.

In 1924 the station staff comprised a station master, booking clerk, two leading porters, one goods yard porter, one goods shed porter, and two junior porters. One of the junior porters from Yate travelled by freight train to Tytherington to collect wagon numbers, also folded the wagon sheets there and brought them back. In the 1950s he went to Iron Acton on the Yate station bicycle and tried to time his visit so that he could bring the cycle back on a train. Messrs Marcroft had an employee stationed at Yate to repair Tytherington quarry stone wagons.

In 1951 the staff at Yate station consisted of a station master, chief clerk, two goods clerks, two passenger clerks, two leading porters and two junior porters. Where two men were provided for a post, one was on early, and the other, the late turn. There were two lorry drivers.

During cold weather the waiting room always had a welcoming coal fire which had just burnt through by the time workers from Parnall's nearby factory and a few from Newman Industries arrived on their homeward journey. The quantity of coal allocated to the station was insufficient, but unofficial supplementary supplies could be obtained from helpful footplatemen.

The station garden won a number of prizes in the mid-1930s. In the late 1950s, wishing to recreate this achievement, the station master requisitioned for gardening tools. These came from Clifton Junction, Manchester, which had no more use for them. The annual inspection for the Best Kept Station award involved the inspector running his fingers along obscure ledges in the waiting room for any trace of dust. The station toilets were always in pristine condition; the fire buckets full of clean water; brass door knobs gleaming and the Courtier stoves black-leaded. The windows were all cleaned thoroughly and no smears left on the glass. Although the platform edges were always kept whitened, they were always given fresh treatment before the inspection. Once again Yate won prizes.

Yate issued workmen's and season tickets for Parnall's factory which from *circa* 1942 ran an assisted travel scheme - workmen could purchase at a discount Early Morning Returns for use before 8.00 am, while the office staff could buy weekly season tickets. The latter were almost unique as normal season tickets issued to women were marked with a 'W', but it was not possible in this case because the tickets were issued by Parnall's. At the peak of the scheme's popularity, each week about 150 tickets were issued to Temple Meads; 60 to

Class '2P' 4-4-0 No. 525 at Yate with a down stopping train *c.*1910. A strong east wind is blowing.
Author's Collection

The Royal Flying Corps on Yate down platform *c.*1916. *Lens of Sutton*

Yate, view up 11th May, 1961. Electric platform lighting has just been installed, but the oil lamps are still in use at this date. Notice the Brunelian architecture.

Author

Class '4' compound 4-4-0 No. 40917 of 21B (Bournville) arriving at Yate with the 1.05 pm Gloucester to Bristol (Temple Meads) stopping train, 18th September, 1951. Notice the wagon turntable and goods shed.

Colin Roberts

View north from Yate station, 2nd January, 1965. Track to the four docks has been lifted and also the crossover to the up main line. Yate Main Line signal box can be seen beyond the bridge.
D. Payne

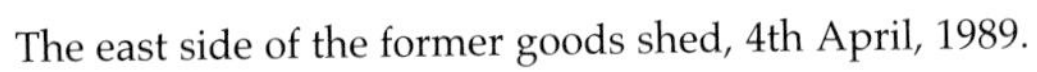

The east side of the former goods shed, 4th April, 1989. *Author*

Yate view down 1935. Notice the sidings radiating from the wagon turntable. *Miles Davey*

Some of the Yate staff on the down platform on 18th May, 1955: booking clerk Colin Roberts, *left*; leading porter Peter Wyatt, *centre*; junior porter Griffith Williams, *right*. *Colin Roberts*

Some of the Yate station staff, October 1960. *Left to right*: leading porter Howard Searle; Colin Roberts, clerk; and shunter Tony Vaisey. *Colin Roberts*

The GWR had running powers over the line through Yate. Here in BR times, 4-6-0 No. 5022 *Wigmore Castle* heads the 10.35 am Wolverhampton (Low Level) to Penzance past a wagon of swarf, 15th August, 1951.
Colin Roberts

Signalman Wilfred Gregory, *far left*, leans from Yate Main Line signal box, 18th April, 1952.
Colin Roberts

Class '3F' 0-6-0 No. 43339 of 21A (Saltley) shed at Yate Main Line signal box on a freight to Westerleigh, 12th October, 1951. The hopper wagons could be part of a new batch branded: 'Return to Tytherington'. Nearly four years after Nationalisation, 'LMS' is still in gold lettering on the tender which is low on coal. The open wagon, right, is loaded with swarf for a South Wales destination. Scrap metal could only be loaded in wooden-bodied trucks; if of steel, the unloading magnet would pick up the entire wagon! *Colin Roberts*

'Jubilee' class 4-6-0 No 45699 *Galatea* of 22A (Bristol, Barrow Road), with a down express passes Yate goods yard in June 1953. Notice on the left the Machine Siding and loading gauge. The weighbridge hut is immediately behind the left-hand buffer. *Colin Roberts*

View on 2nd January, 1965 north from the road overbridge at Yate. To the left of Yate Main Line signal box double track diverges to the Thornbury branch; wagons on the left stand on the siding known as the 'pawn shop' because wagons were stored there; the loading dock is on the right several trailers stand in the yard and Parnall's (Yate) Ltd's factory is beyond. *D. Payne*

'Patriot' class 4-6-0 No. 45509 *The Derbyshire Yeomanry* heads the down Nottingham to Bristol express. Class '4F' 0-6-0 No. 44355 is shunting before working a train to Thornbury on 17th August, 1956. *Author*

Class '2P' 4-4-0 No. 40423 of 22B (Gloucester), approaches Yate on 18th April, 1952 working the 7.42 am Gloucester to Bristol (Temple Meads). In Parnall's siding, right, a van awaits unloading. On the left are coaches which had formed the 8.20 am Bristol to Yate which mainly carried Parnall's office staff. This train formerly ran through to Thornbury. *Colin Roberts*

From the footplate of class '8F' 2-8-0 No. 48003, working an up ballast train in April 1964, can be seen vans standing in Messrs Parnall's siding. A ballast cleaner is on the down road.
W.F. Grainger

Staple Hill; 60 to Fishponds; 20 to Mangotsfield, Warmley, Oldland Common and Bitton; about 10 to Charfield and 2 for Wickwar - in total over 300 tickets issued weekly. The factory had a night, as well as day, shift.

In its earlier days Yate was used by the well-heeled. Before the Wootton Bassett to Filton line was opened via Badminton, Yate saw some of the Duke of Beaufort's guests, the Prince and Princess of Wales entraining at Yate after a triumphant journey from Badminton in an open horse-drawn carriage.

Since the closure of Yate station to passenger traffic on 4th January, 1965, the community has developed as a new town and its increased population of approximately 20,000 called for the station to be re-opened. The platforms of pink interlocking bricks are completely new - No. 2, the down platform placed north of the overbridge and No. 1, the up platform, to the south and approximately on the site of the original. Avon County Council footed the bill of £140,000. The plastic seats in the waiting shelters are weighted so that they automatically return to a vertical position when sitters rise. Both platforms have adjacent free car parks. The station was officially re-opened by Councillor Warren Fowler on 11th May, 1989 and the occasion marked by a plaque. Public opening was four days later, the first train leaving for Bristol at 7.17 am. A feeder bus from Chipping Sodbury and North Yate met almost every arrival and departure. The forecast of station usage was 150 to 340 journeys per day and a survey in November 1989 showed a figure of just under 300. Daily usage in 2001 varies between 200 and 260, with 10 trains each way Mondays-Fridays and 8 up and 7 down on Saturdays. From June 1990 the feeder bus service was extended to Hawkesbury Upton and Horton. In 1991 a ramp for the disabled was built at a cost of £70,000, this sum being shared by Avon County Council and British Rail. At a further cost of £125,000, the platforms were extended to take a 4-car train. There is now a ticket sales kiosk on the down platform, open Mondays to Fridays from 6.30 until 10.00 am. The 10th anniversary of the re-opening of the station was celebrated on 20th March, 1999 when preserved BR Standard class '4' 2-6-4T No. 80079 worked a special from Bristol (Temple Meads) with a rake of six coaches. It made three shuttle trips between Yate and Tytherington.

On 4th April, 1989 a view north from the new up platform at Yate with the former goods shed, right, and the new down platform on the far side of the bridge. *Author*

The new up platform before the shelter was erected. Viewed from the down platform, 4th April, 1989. *Author*

On 4th April, 1989 a view north from the overbridge before the erection of a shelter on the new down platform at Yate. *Author*

Provincial Manager, Western
British Rail, 125 House
1 Gloucester Street Swindon SN1 1DL
Telephone 0793-26100. Telex 299431 SWGM

y/r:
o.r:CP4/PROV/89

Date:25.04.89

Dear Mr. Wake

RE-OPENING OF YATE STATION
THURSDAY MAY 11 1989

I have great pleasure in inviting you to join us at Yate on Thursday May 11 when a plaque to mark the re-opening of the station will be unveiled by Councillor Warren Fowler, Chairman, Avon County Council.

Thereafter we will board an inaugural special train to Bristol Temple Meads where we will be the guests of Avon County Council for lunch.

The plaque will be unveiled at 11.00 followed by a short tour of the facilities. The train will leave for Bristol at 11.45 and a coach will be provided for those guests wishing to return to Yate station.

Yours sincerely

John Pearse

RE-OPENING OF YATE STATION
THURSDAY MAY 11 1989

I shall/shall not be able to attend

I shall be represented by

Name________________ Address____________________

Guests are reminded that the nearest Railway station for Yate until May 15 is Bristol Parkway. Should you require a rail ticket please indicate your point of departure.________________

For further information telephone Ioan James 0793 515475.

Yate

Station Re-Opening

British Rail
wish to welcome you aboard the
inaugural train between

Yate and Bristol Temple Meads

Thursday May 11 1989

This ticket is issued subject to the conditions shown in the British Railways Board's current Conditions of Carriage of Passengers and their Luggage and also in any other of the board's Publications or notices appropriate to its use. It is not transferable.

Invitation ticket for Yate's inaugural service to Bristol (Temple Meads), 11th May, 1989.

The incorrect re-opening plaque.
Author

The correct re-opening plaque.
Author

The bill board on the down platform at Yate. Passengers awaiting the first train from the re-opened station, 15th May, 1989. *Author*

Yate station information point, 24th August, 2000. *Author*

Yate: the arrival of the first service train, the 6.52 am Gloucester to Bristol (Temple Meads), worked by No. 150 247, 15th May, 1989. The Tytherington branch is on the left. *Author*

The ticket sales kiosk on the down platform, Yate, 24th August, 2000. *Author*

The Thornbury branch ran north-westwards from Yate Main Line Junction signal box round a 13 chain radius curve and was double for a quarter of a mile to Yate Single Line Junction signal box. In the fork formed by the branch and the main line, was a locomotive turntable, but this was removed by 1905 as it saw little use because trains from the branch ran southwards. A siding parallel with the down branch line was often used for storing coaches.

Level at first, after half a mile the line falls at 1 in 176. Immediately before Iron Acton station was a signal box where the branch to Frampton Cotterell diverged. From Iron Acton Junction the Frampton branch turned almost 180 degrees on a 15 chain radius curve before crossing the River Frome and terminating on an embankment due east of the parish church, a mile from the junction. Bridges on this short line were constructed for double track, though only single was laid. According to the working timetable trains ceased running by 1st February, 1877, but closure of the branch was not authorised until 15th April, 1878. The track was lifted in 1892, except for a short length left as Iron Acton goods siding. As recently as 1939 three occupation level crossings were complete with gates and Midland Railway plates, and some boundary posts could be found. Apart from earthworks there is little other trace today.

Frampton Cotterell iron ore was like red-coloured stone, but felt heavy when compared with ordinary stone. Thousands of tons were dug between 1862 and 1874, the chief pits being Burgess, Red Gin and Roden Acre. The ore was dispatched for smelting at Seend and Westbury in Wiltshire, and to South Wales. Before the branch was opened the ore was dispatched from Yate, the Chillington Iron Co., which owned the mines 1862-3, having its own wagons as did the Frampton Haematite Co. Although the ore was of good quality, water seepage into the workings became a problem and in 1874 when the pits became full of water, mining ceased.

Tonnages of Iron Ore Extracted at Frampton Cotterell

Year	*Number of Tons*	*Owner*
1869	6,773	Frampton Haematite Co.
1870	15,249	Frampton Haematite Co.
1871	8,487	(Uncertain ownership)
1872	9,201	Brogden & Sons
1873	13,682	Brogden & Sons
1874	14,842	Brogden & Sons

In 1884 the West Gloucestershire Water Co. took over the Roden Acre shaft and extracted water using a beam engine. The supply is now used by Bristol Waterworks.

In 1902 part of the Frampton branch was relaid for use by the Tytherington Stone Co., but taken out of use in March 1907. The siding was finally closed on 10th June, 1963 and lifted the following November. It had been used as a coal depot only from 19th June, 1944. The Co-op was required to have all the remaining coal cleared from its standing ground by 19th June, 1964.

Iron Acton level crossing had a pair of gates, one left open to form the entrance to the goods yard and weighbridge. As the siding diverged on the Yate

The station builder's sign with the junction beyond, 4th April, 1989. *Author*

Yate Middle ground frame, 4th April, 1989. *Author*

Class '4F' 0-6-0 No. 44296 with a train from Thornbury about to join the main line at Yate, September 1963. *W.F. Grainger*

Yate Junction from cab of HST power car No. 43015 working the 6.25 am Plymouth to Newcastle, 11th May, 1991. *Author*

An unusual design of skew bridge over the River Frome at Yate Single Line Junction, 14th February, 2001. *Author*

The underline bridge on the Yate to Engine Common road on 10th April, 1991. Originally of double track width, it was rebuilt only for single line. *Author*

The original bridge on the Yate to Engine Common road was similar to the one shown here.
Author

A dumb buffer wagon belonging to the Chillington Iron Company, Iron Mines, Yate. Note its wooden brake blocks.
Author's Collection

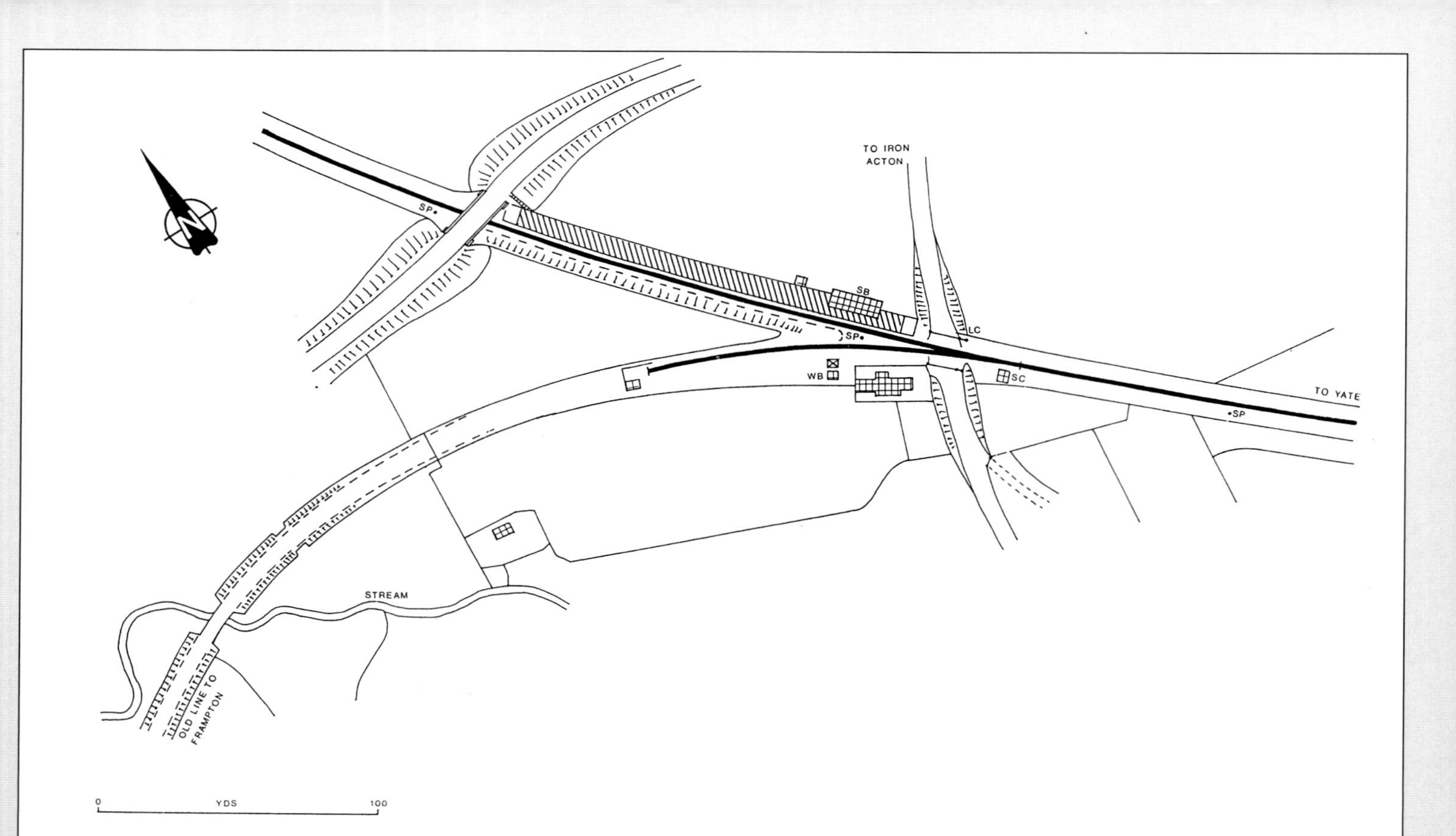

1922
IRON ACTON

side of the crossing, there was double track across the lane which disadvantaged road traffic as a train shunting blocked the highway. As this siding had facing points, it could only be shunted on a return journey from Thornbury unless unauthorised fly shunting was employed, or a wagon was pushed from Yate in front of the engine. For demurrage purposes, the late turn junior passenger porter at Yate was responsible for taking details of wagons containing coal at Iron Acton, noting the wagon numbers of those empty at the close of work.

The single platform Iron Acton station, situated on the south side of the line, had a moderate-sized timber building. The platform itself, like the others on the branch, was a stone support wall retaining a bank of earth topped with a gravel surface. Later they received a coating of tarmac. During World War II the station was staffed by a female, but unstaffed by 1946. The station building was demolished *circa* 1960.

At 2 miles 8 chains, from 1972 there was a level crossing over the new Iron Acton by-pass (*see page 69*). The original track formation fell at 1 in 135 to Latteridge level crossing at 2 miles 47 chains. Latteridge, or Laddenridge, means a ridge of high ground above the valley of the Ladden Brook. A platelayer lived in the crossing cottage and his wife opened the gates. A down train whistled when leaving Iron Acton crossing to warn of its approach to Latteridge.

On 22nd August, 1956 class '4F' 0-6-0 No. 44424 approaches Iron Acton station with a train from Thornbury. Twelve years after the cessation of passenger traffic, the station is still in good order. To avoid paying rates the platform edging stones have been removed. A chicken run has been established on the platform beyond the station building. *Author*

Iron Acton station *c.*1930, view towards Thornbury. The level crossing is in the foreground and the erstwhile branch to Frampton Cotterell, now a siding, curves left. A trap point can be seen to the right of the pedal car's bonnet. *Author's Collection*

In 1964 class '4F' 0-6-0 No. 44466 on Iron Acton crossing *en route* to Yate. The former crossing keeper's lodge is on the left. The Frampton branch curved left. *W.F. Grainger*

View of the remains of Iron Acton platform from the footplate of class '4F' 0-6-0 No. 44296, *en route* to Yate in September 1963. It has stopped for the fireman to get down and open the gates. *W.F. Grainger*

Fireman Royston Tucker closes Iron Acton crossing gates to road traffic while No. 44296 simmers in the background, September 1963. *W.F. Grainger*

Iron Acton station *c.*1960, the station buildings have been demolished. *Lens of Sutton*

No. 44296 waits beyond Iron Acton crossing for the guard to open the gates to road traffic, September 1963. *W.F. Grainger*

Class '4F' 0-6-0 No. 44466 *en route* to Thornbury, approaches Latteridge crossing in 1964.
W.F. Grainger

View north to Latteridge crossing from the cab of class '4F' 0-6-0 No. 44466. This 1963 view shows clearly that the formation was built wide enough for double track. *W.F. Grainger*

A car on Latteridge crossing, March 1964 as seen from a '4F'. *W.F. Grainger*

Fireman Royston Tucker opens the gates at Latteridge to allow class '4F' 0-6-0 No. 44296 to pass with an up train, September 1963. *W.F. Grainger*

The line undulates and on the west side of the line immediately behind Ladden Brook, between Tytherington No. 1 ground frame at 4 miles 19 chains and No. 2 ground frame at 4 miles 41 chains, the Admiralty Stone Siding holding 60 wagons was brought into use on 25th August, 1918. Latterly referred to as 'Latteridge Loop' it was utilised for storing coaching stock. Due to the steep gradient, all wagons for Tytherington station and the quarry sidings conveyed by down trains were required to be taken in front of the engine from this loop.

From No. 2 ground frame the line rose at 1 in 61 to Tytherington station, 5 miles 10 chains and identical in design to that at Iron Acton. It was situated on an embankment on the north-east side of the track. In 1946 it was staffed by a leading porter, the post of station master having been abolished following the withdrawal of the passenger service in 1944. Station repairs cost 6*s*. 9*d*. in 1946, £1 7*s*. 3*d*. in 1947 and £1 0*s*. 6*d*. in 1948. From 1st August, 1949 the station became unstaffed and closed to parcels, from that date items being collected and delivered from Yate. A Boy Scout troop held the tenancy of the building from 1949 until the branch closed in 1967. Construction of the railway cut across the garden of Porch House, West Street, leaving a detached strip of 1½ acres on the west side of the line. This was purchased from the owners of Porch House and The Villa built on it.

North of the station at 5 miles 21 chains, from 1884 a siding led into West Quarry. The siding closed on 10th June, 1963 and was taken out of use that October. From 29th August, 1898 on the opposite side of the branch, a siding led to Church Quarry.

The gradient rises at 1 in 59/61 through a tree-lined cutting where difficulties are experienced in the autumn due to fallen leaves. The cutting's steep sides are secured by stone pitching. Apart from the two summit tunnels and the cuttings at their ends, earthworks on the branch were light.

The 224 yds-long Tytherington tunnel begins at 5 miles 46 chains and ends at 5 miles 56 chains. It has a red brick southern portal and the tunnel is lined only at the ends. At one period it had a ventilation shaft, but this was subsequently bricked over. In June 1956 15 tons of rock fell from the roof and caused the line to be closed for a week. Today the railway tunnel is horizontally sandwiched between the M5 above and an unlined private road tunnel taking 50 tonne lorries between Grovesend and Woodlease quarries. Just outside the railway tunnel snails could be found on a wall. One driver collected them, placed them on the back of the firebox and when cooked, prised their flesh out with a safety pin.

The line emerges from the tunnel into Grovesend (or Tytherington) Quarry. The siding serving it was originally brought into use on 26th June, 1888 for Hardwicke Lloyd, Hardwicke being the local squire. The quarry later became part of Roads Reconstruction (1934) Limited's empire but today it is owned by Hanson. Rail facilities consist of a loop, loading taking place on the right-hand road, the left being used for run-round purposes. Three short terminal sidings were provided for crippled wagons, but are no longer in regular use and at the time of writing are covered with stock pile. Beyond the loader, the line falls at 1 in 58 towards Thornbury. Today it ends at 6 miles 23 chains, but the headshunt beyond the north end of the run-round loop (6 miles 2 chains) is very overgrown.

Grovesend tunnel, 167 yards in length and lined throughout, is now blocked. Beyond was a descent of 1 in 50 through a limestone cutting in which were good

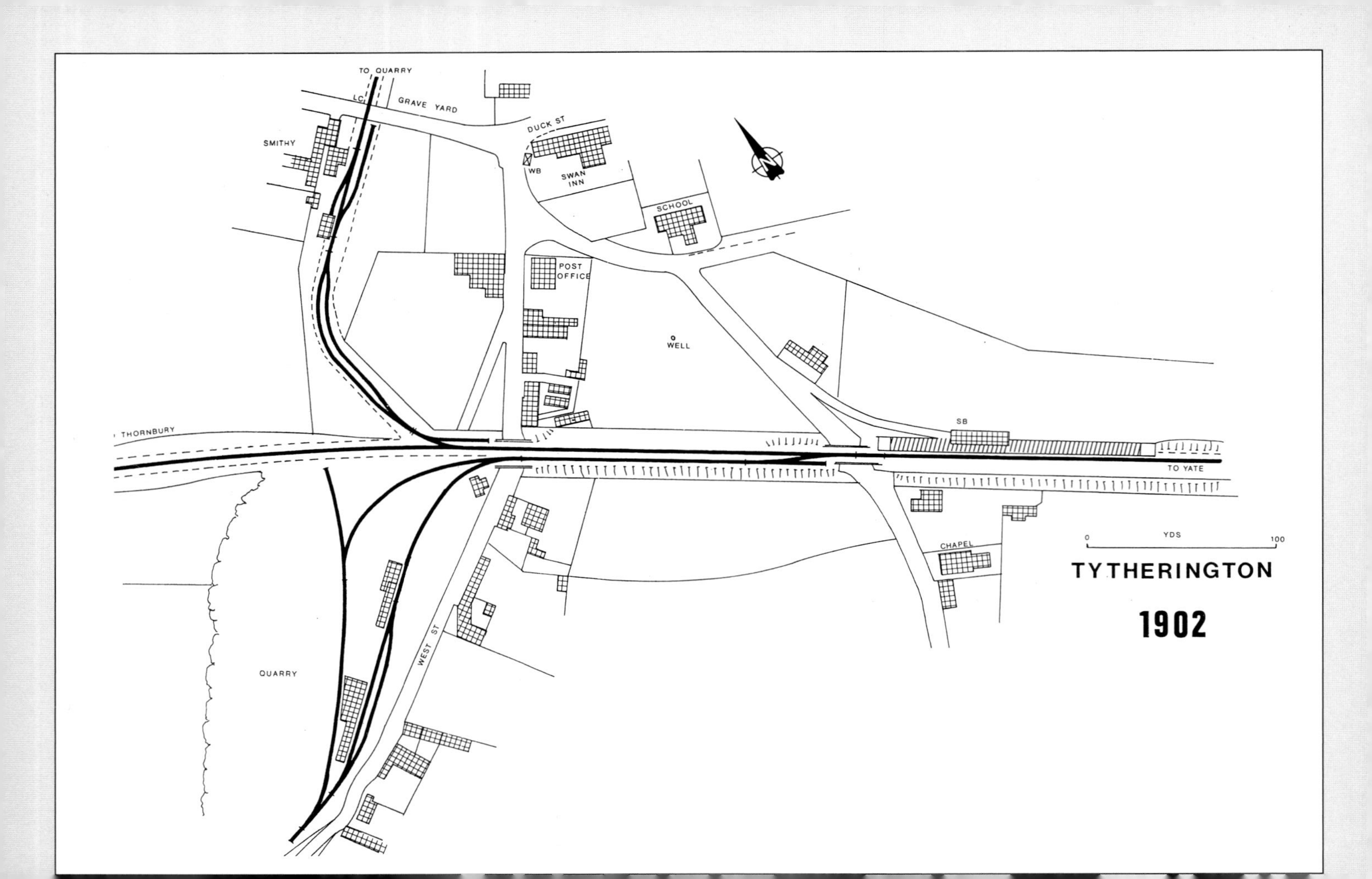
TO QUARRY
LC
GRAVE YARD
DUCK ST
SMITHY
WB
SWAN INN
SCHOOL
POST OFFICE
WELL
SB
THORNBURY
TO YATE
QUARRY
WEST ST
CHAPEL
0
YDS
100
TYTHERINGTON
1902

Class '4F' 0-6-0 No. 44466 with a train to Thornbury, approaches the site of Tytherington station in April 1964. *W.F. Grainger*

Tytherington station 22nd August, 1956, view towards Iron Acton. *Author*

Former station master's house at Tytherington, 10th April 1991.
Author

Tytherington station, view north *c.*1960. The goods siding is on the left beyond the far end of the platform. *Lens of Sutton*

In March 1964 class '4F' 0-6-0 No. 44534 heads an up train past the formation of Tytherington siding, taken out of use in October 1963. *W.F. Grainger*

Class '4F' 0-6-0 No. 44466 about to enter Tytherington tunnel with a down train in April 1964.
W.F. Grainger

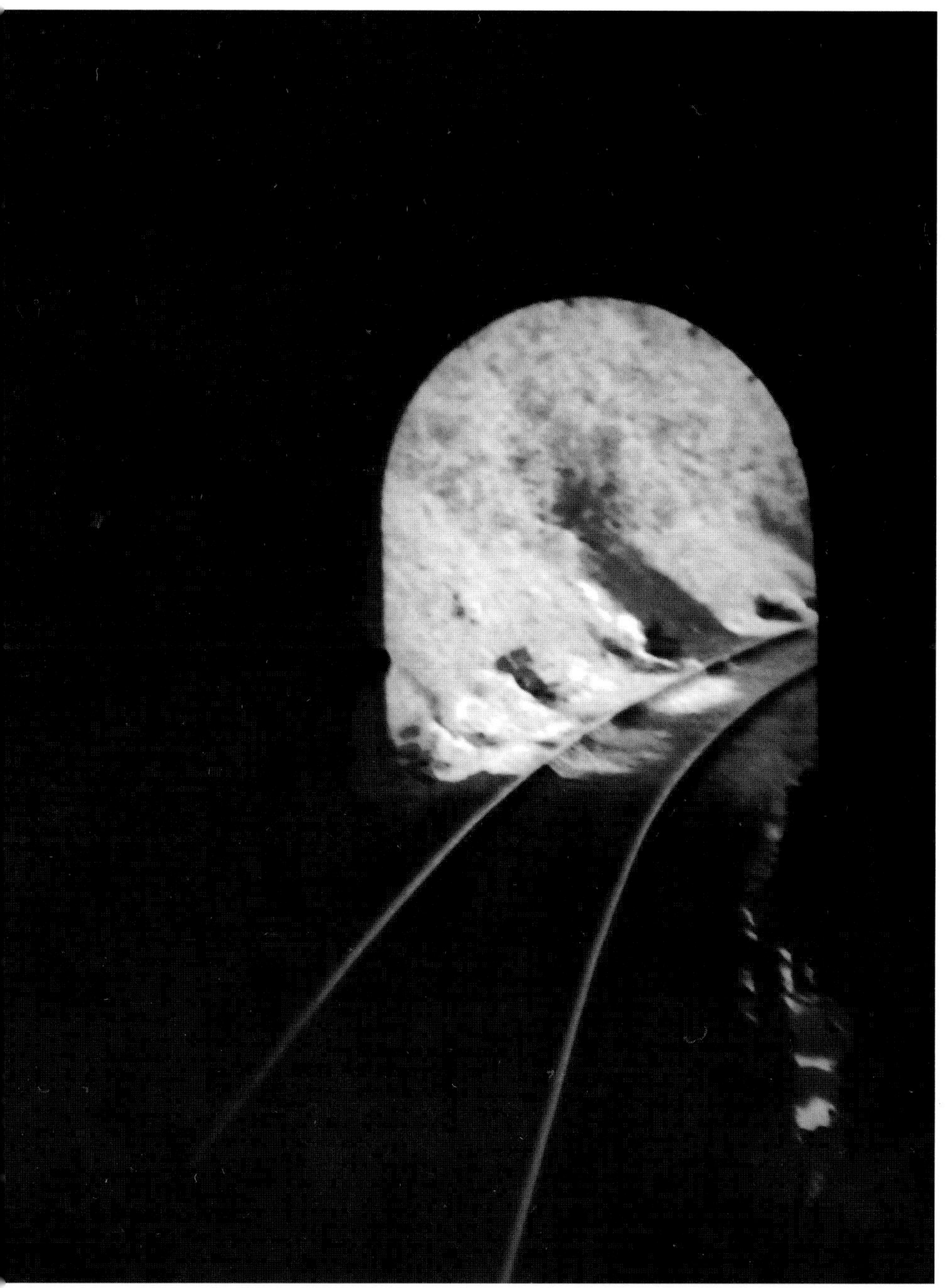

View from the cab of No. 44466 to the east portal of Tytherington tunnel, April 1964.
W.F. Grainger

The attractive bridge carrying a minor road across the railway north of Tytherington Quarry, 10th April, 1991. *Author*

Class '4F' 0-6-0 No. 44466 approaches the southern end of Grovesend tunnel in April 1964. Notice the aqueduct which crosses the line. The bridge beyond the aqueduct carrying the A38 bears the cast-iron plate No. 17. The tunnel is immediately beyond. *W.F. Grainger*

watercress beds. On at least one occasion in damp, foggy weather, a class '4F' 0-6-0 climbing from Thornbury with only three or four wagons, slipped to a standstill on this gradient when its sanders proved inoperative. The branch approached the terminus at Thornbury by passing over an embankment from which a wide vista of the Severn was obtained.

Thornbury station, 7 miles 31 chains, had a neat, stone, typical Midland Railway twin-pavilion style building with freestone dressings and elaborate fretted barge boards and a roof which was tiled, rather than slated, as were most of the similar examples of this type. The single platform had a run-round loop. There were three sidings, a stone-built goods shed, cattle loading dock unused after 1956, and 1½ ton crane. The dock for wheeled traffic was last used in the early 1960s when a vehicle for HM Prison, Leyhill, arrived from the Ministry of Supply siding, Ruddington, Notts.

Station staff in 1941 consisted of a station master, two clerks, two porters, and two passenger guards. Arthur Knapp was the London, Midland & Scottish Railway (LMS) carter and used either a four-wheeled dray with pneumatic tyres, or if carrying perishables and it was wet, he used the four-wheeled covered van with wooden wheels and iron tyres. His horse was stabled in High Street at 'The Exchange' public house, now known as the 'Knot of Rope'. His post ceased on 28th August, 1946 when zonal collection and delivery commenced with a lorry based at Yate and by the end of that year, staff at Thornbury were just a station master and one porter.

'4F' class 0-6-0 No. 44466 approaches Thornbury ground frame hut in 1964.

W.F. Grainger

Thornbury Station Building

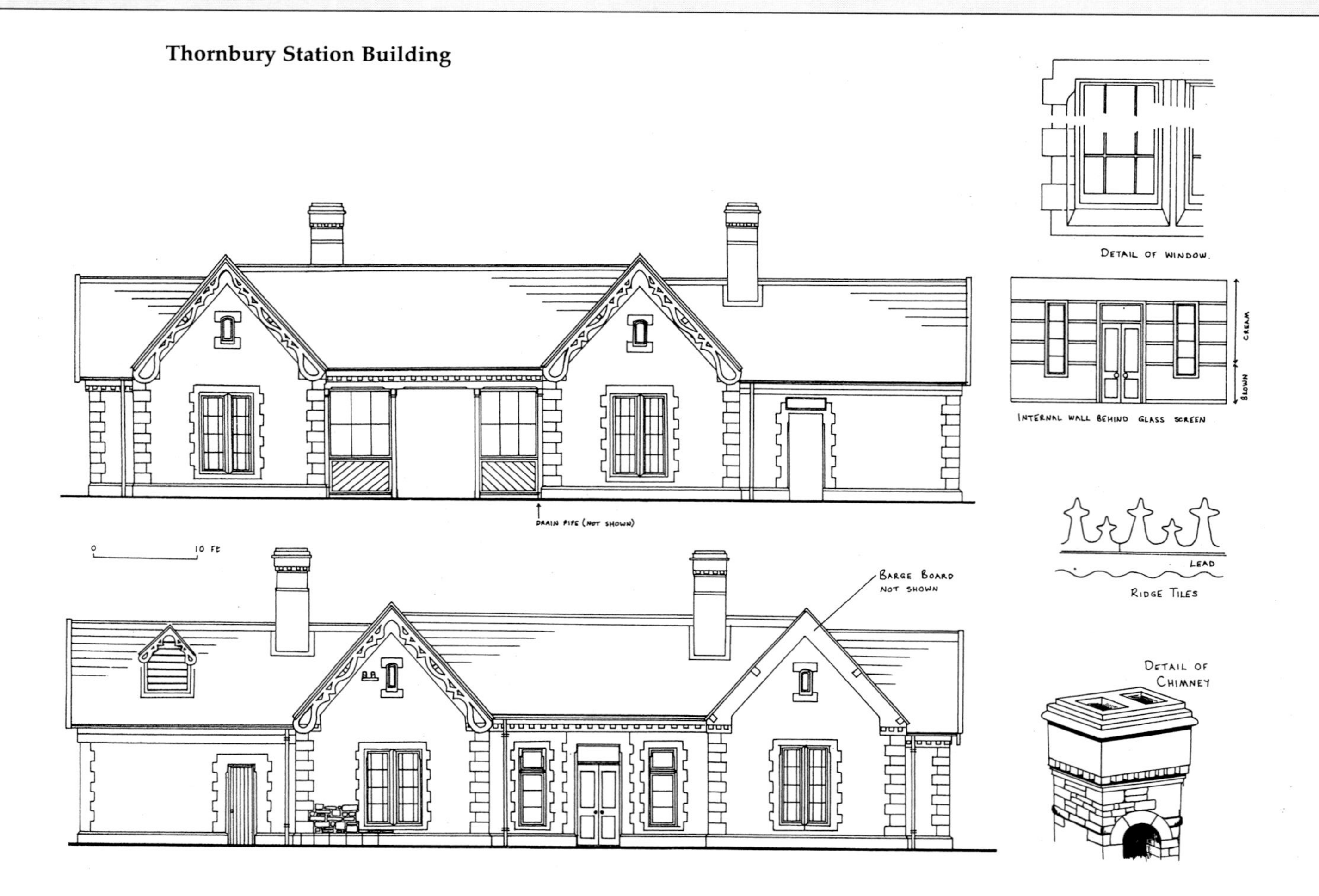

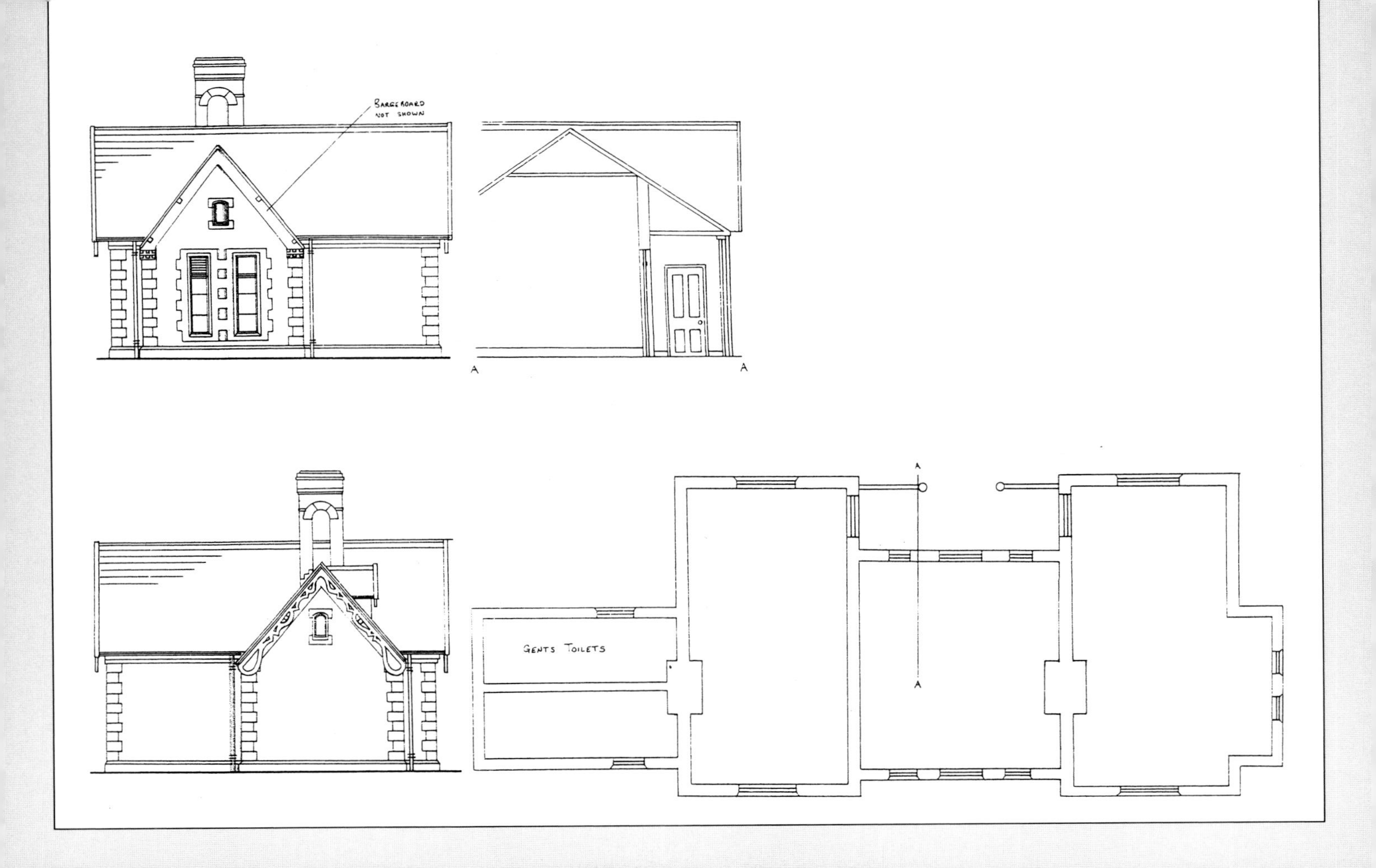
BARGEBOARD NOT SHOWN
A
A
A
A
GENTS TOILETS

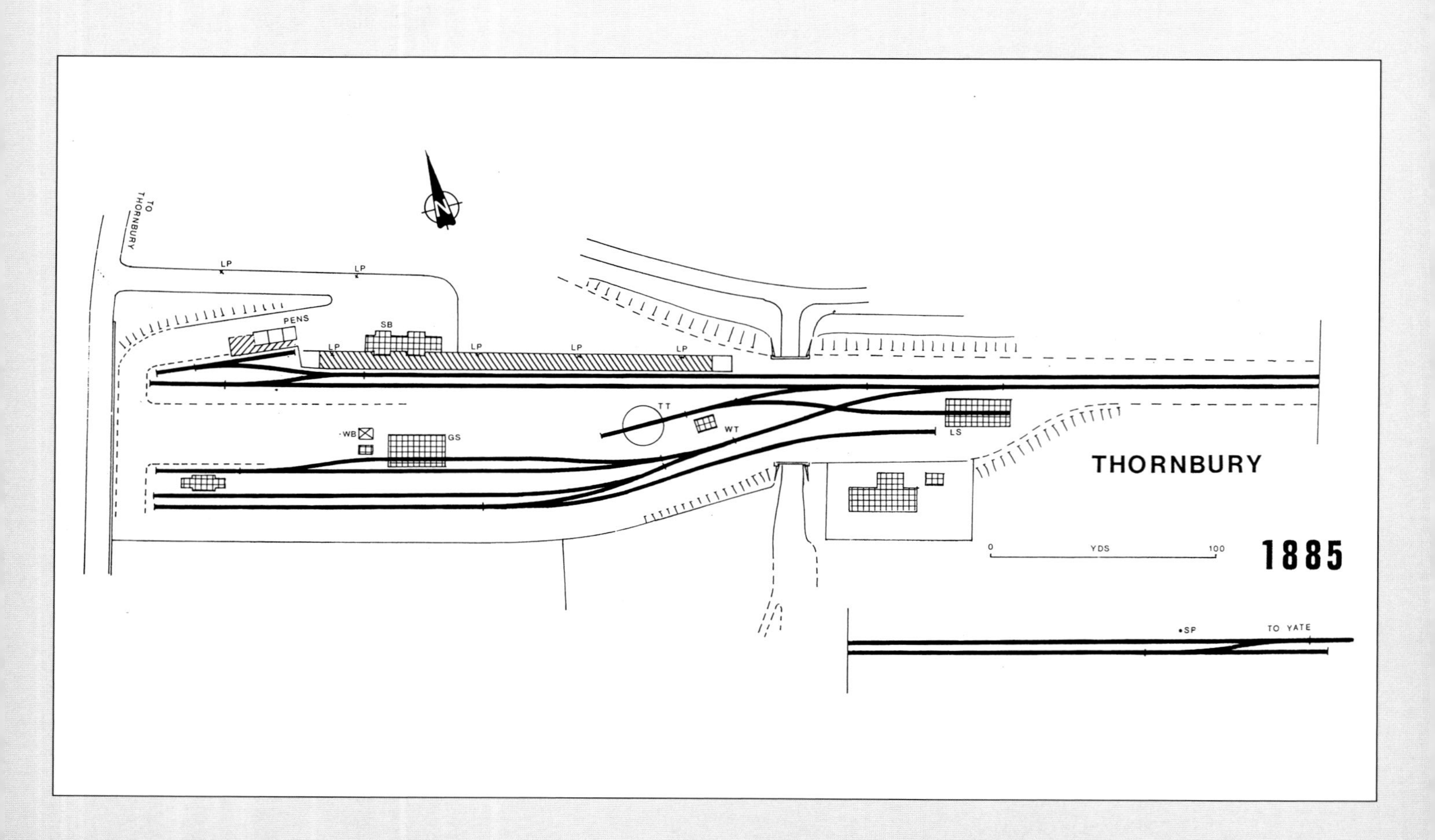
THORNBURY
1885
0
YDS
100
TO THORNBURY
TO YATE
SP
LP
LP
LP
LP
LP
LP
PENS
SB
TT
WT
WB
GS
LS
N

View along the platform at Thornbury to the blocks from the cab of class '4F' No. 44569, 82E (Bristol, Barrow Road), 25th October, 1963. *W.F. Grainger*

Sam Collins, the Thornbury porter, and Caradoc Williams, the Yate station master, at Thornbury station, 17th August, 1956. The cattle pens and loading dock are to the left of the station building. *Author*

Thornbury station, 5th January, 1952. *Author's Collection*

General view of Thornbury yard in 1963. The Coles crane is unloading steel while the Ransome-Rapier crane is standing spare. *W.F. Grainger*

In 1964 class '4F' 0-6-0 No. 44466, 82E, stands at Thornbury ready to depart. To its left a 'Presflo' wagon stands outside the goods shed. *W.F. Grainger*

Class '4F' 0-6-0 No. 44534 of 82E near Thornbury goods shed in 1962. The chalked instruction 'Do not move' is not meant to be obeyed here. *W.F. Grainger*

A 1964 view from Thornbury yard looking up the bank towards Grovesend tunnel from the cab of No. 44466. The engine shed is on the right. *W.F. Grainger*

Thornbury engine shed, loco coal and ash wagons, *c.*1935. *Author's Collection*

One day in the 1950s a fleet of road coaches parked in the station yard while their drivers took lunch time refreshment. Apparently their operator had gone into liquidation and the vehicles were being moved to the North. The station master was unhappy with the situation as no one had asked permission to park the coaches there, so he decided to make a charge. When the drivers came to remove the coaches, one of them, in reversing, dropped a wheel into the turntable well. The coalman who worked from the yard, started filling the well with sleepers so that the coach could be extricated, but before they had raised them to a sufficient height to release the coach, a train arrived and its engine needed turning. In addition to the parking fee, the station master charged for locomotive waiting time.

During the 1950s and 1960s, the station kept a £1 float for change. Colin Roberts, the Yate booking clerk, was responsible for maintaining the inwards and outwards records and travelled there weekly to collect the receipts from the safe to pay in with the Yate revenue. It was deposited in a travelling safe which went to Fishponds and the station master there paid it into a local bank. Wages cash came from a travelling safe on a Worcester to Bristol train, a railway policeman riding with it in the van.

Repairs of Thornbury station were required to be within an annual limit of £10. In 1946 the sum spent was £1 16*s*. 8*d*.; in 1947 £6 4*s*. 11*d*. and in 1948 12*s*. 0*d*. Items needing replacement included a Roman tile, glass, putty, a lavatory seat and plumbing. The station ladders had to be tested quarterly. The method was to lay them horizontally close to the ground and two men made a practical test. Each rung was required to be struck on each side with a 1½ lb. hammer. Tall steps, or tower ladders, were tested by the District Engineer.

The site of Thornbury station is now covered by industrial units.

The former engine shed and view up the bank towards Grovesend tunnel from the cab of No. 44466 in 1964. *W.F. Grainger*

BRISTOL 809

(Extract frum Bristol 69)

1700 H.P. Diesel

Enginemen

Bath Road

809A 0510 to 1310 **MO**
809A 0440 **MX** to 1240 **WFO**, 1318 **TThO**, 1310 **SO**
809B 1014 to 1905 **SX**
809C 1425 to 2005 **SO**

	arr.	dep.	
Bath Road Depot ..		05‖45	**LD MO**
Stoke Gifford	06‖15		
Avonmouth (R.E. Yard)		06‖00	**LD MX**
Stoke Gifford	06‖15		
(Diesel off 2335 Weymouth **MX**)			
Stoke Gifford		0630	**9F38 D**
Yate	0655 **Shunt**		
Yate		09†00	**EBV MWFO**
Rangeworthy	09†09	09†16	**EBV Water cans**
Yate	09†26	0935	**9B25 Q**
Mangotsfield	0950 **h**	1050	**9C88**
Yate	1120		

h—Reverse and Shunt Engineers Dept. Traffic.

	arr.	dep.	
Yate		1130	**9F38 MWFO**
Grovesend	**R**		
Thornbury	1210	1230	**9F38**
Grovesend	**R**		
Yate	1310		
Yate		0900	**9F38 TThSO**
Grovesend	0930	0940	
Thornbury	0955	1055	**9F38**
Grovesend	1105	1120	
Yate	1155		
Yate		12‖20	**LE SO**
Bath Road Depot ..	12‖50		
Yate		1330	**9F38 SX**
Grovesend	1400	1410	
Thornbury	1425	1500	**9F38**
Grovesend	1510	1540	
Yate	1610 **Shunt**		
Yate		1722	**9C68**
Stoke Gifford	1810	18‖15	**LD**
Bath Road Depot ..	18‖45		
Bath Road Depot ..		15‖00	**LD SO**
Stoke Gifford	15‖30	1545	**9B07**
North Somerset Junction		16*35	
St. Philip's Marsh ..	1652		
West Depot	1705	17‖15	**LD**
Dr. Day's Sidings ..	17‖25	19†30	**ECS**
(for 2025 to Leeds)			
Bristol (T.M.)	19†35	19‖40	**LD**
Bath Road Depot ..	19‖45		

Working timetables 6th September, 1965-17th April, 1966.

Chapter Three

Closure and Re-Opening

Thornbury station closed to freight traffic on 20th June, 1966 and on this day the trip engine arrived as usual with plenty of traffic for the closed stations - someone had omitted to inform the Operating and Locomotive Departments of the closure! Although shut to other types of goods traffic, stone trains continued to run from Grovesend Quarry. With the termination of the private siding agreement on 30th September, 1967 the Thornbury branch was 'closed', but due to a new stone contract, traffic continued until 24th November, 1967. Several weeks after this, five wagons of granite for Tytherington Quarry arrived at Stoke Gifford marshalling yard from Coalville, Leicestershire. As Stoke Gifford did not have the requisite facilities, through the good offices of the proprietor, the 21 ton hopper wagons were unloaded at Filton Coal Concentration Depot, the contents falling down the coal chutes into an Amalgamated Roadstone Corporation (ARC) lorry. This granite was part of an irregular flow of traffic, the granite being mixed at Tytherington with local stone.

Thomas Ward began track recovery of the Thornbury branch in September 1968 and type '3' Beyer, Peacock diesel-hydraulic 'Hymeks' Nos. D7041 and D7012 were noted with the lifting train on 6th and 7th September respectively; subsequently a North British type '2' diesel-hydraulic of the 'D63XX' class also appeared. However, this track-lifting did not prove to be the end of the story. In 1968-69 Tytherington Quarry (an alternative name for Grovesend Quarry), was being developed to prepare for the construction of the M5 in 1970-1. Grovesend Quarry had reached its boundaries in the mid-1960s and North Quarry, on the other side of the Tytherington to Grovesend road, opened in 1964 with material being transported across the public road into the plant area at Grovesend Quarry. In 1969 communications were improved when a tunnel was driven below the highway to carry the stone directly to the new plant.

In 1970 Stephen Savery, Area Director of ARC owners of the quarry, looked ahead for markets when the contract for supplying roadstone for the Almondsbury to Tewkesbury length of the M5 had been fulfilled. In addition to being an excellent roadstone, Tytherington aggregate had been used in high quality concrete such as concrete abutments and anchorages for the first Severn Bridge, and reactor shields for Oldbury-on-Severn atomic power station.

Ironically for the road transport lobby, the enormous increase in the demand for ordinary road and motorway construction, increased the need to transport more aggregate by rail. Quarry sales are limited by radius, for in the case of road haulage, the price for a market over 10 miles distant causes the price to be doubled, but rail transport enables the limit to be extended up to 100 miles, so accessible markets can cover an area 100 times as great.

Stephen Savery realised that a rail link would open two categories of market: (a) permanent railhead depots situated in high growth centres and (b) temporary railheads for major construction projects. It was agreed that Tytherington would supply stone to ARC customers north of the M4, and New Frome Quarry on the Mendips, to those to the south.

An aerial view of Tytherington Quarry *c.*1970. The M5 motorway is just beyond the far face of the quarry, with the line of the former Thornbury branch curving diagonally across the photograph from lower left to upper right. *Author's Collection*

Savery's letter putting these proposals to the General Manager of British Rail/Western Region (BR/WR) arrived on the very day that the new Iron Acton by-pass was being opened and as the new road crossed the trackbed on the level, it was anticipated that the Department of Transport would be against relaying. Due to the urging and enthusiasm of Kenneth Painter, the WR's assistant divisional manager, this resistance was overcome. Although it was environmentally sound that an 800 tonne train would keep 80 ten-tonne lorries off the road, some householders living near the lifted railway were unhappy about the track being relaid. This resistance was overcome, Tytherington tunnel unsealed, four bridges rebuilt or strengthened, and six miles of track laid together with 20,000 tonnes of ballast. The Eagre Construction Co. won the contract and used its own 0-4-0 diesel-mechanical locomotive *Alfred Henshall*, Ruston, Hornsby No. 313392 built in 1952 and previously used by the North Western Gas Board at Denton, Lancashire. Speed was the hallmark of the relaying operation: it began in mid-April 1972 and the first train ran, its destination Milton Keynes, on 3rd July, 1972 - almost exactly a century after the original opening. Of the five metal underbridges, Nos. 2, 9, 12 and 13 had to be rebuilt and powers that had existed since 1953 were exercised and No. 8 filled in. As the light MR bridge construction was about 9 in. shallower than a modern pre-stressed concrete deck necessary to support 100 tonne wagons having a 25 tonne axle loading, the track had to be raised at each bridge to allow for this work. Fortunately all the masonry bridges were in good condition. A serious problem was that the 10 ft high deck of overbridge No. 13 at West Street, Tytherington, had been removed at the request of the National Farmers' Union to allow milk tankers and cattle lorries to reach a farm. A 13 ft 6 in. headroom was agreed and, with the 9 in. in height mentioned above, the track had to be raised 4 ft 3 in., and at this point the track was on a double width embankment. Unfortunately the alternative of excavating the road was quite out of the question, as solid limestone lay directly beneath the tarred surface and Bristol Waterworks laying a nearby main were seen to be using gelignite cartridges at an expensive rate. The rising gradient of 1 in 59 was replaced by 200 yards of 1 in 42 and then being level for 100 yards before regaining the existing 1 in 59. The necessary fill was brought down by lorry from the quarry half a mile distant as the bridge works needed to be completed before track laying could begin.

At Iron Acton the hitherto falling gradient of 1 in 175 towards Tytherington required modification due to the level crossing over the new by-pass. A new bridge was quite out of the question as it would have cost £400,000. The old, steadily-falling gradient was replaced by 60 ft of track rising at 1 in 30. The crossing of the road was 1 in 24 and the rails had to conform to the road surface, but as they crossed at an angle, the gradient was reduced to 1 in 30. It was followed by a fall to regain the former track level. As this second gradient rose against loaded trains, it was limited to 1 in 135 and thus had to be extended over 600 yards. The gradient north of the Itchington Road overbridge near the north end of Tytherington Quarry run-round loop had to be raised with thousands of tons of stone to ease the descending gradient so that a loaded train could be stabled in the headshunt in order that two trains could cross. The original gradient was too steep for a loaded train to be drawn out. The headshunt today

View of the site of the former Iron Acton station on 21st April, 1972 looking towards the level crossing and crossing keeper's lodge. The trackbed is being prepared for re-laying.
Author's Collection

Tytherington Quarry - the track bed being prepared for relaying, near Tytherington tunnel, 21st April, 1972. The old weighbridge can be seen on the left. *Author's Collection*

An underline bridge at West Street Tytherington which has been raised and strengthened in an insensitive manner, 10th April, 1991. *Author*

Another strengthened underline bridge at Tytherington, 10th April, 1991. *Author*

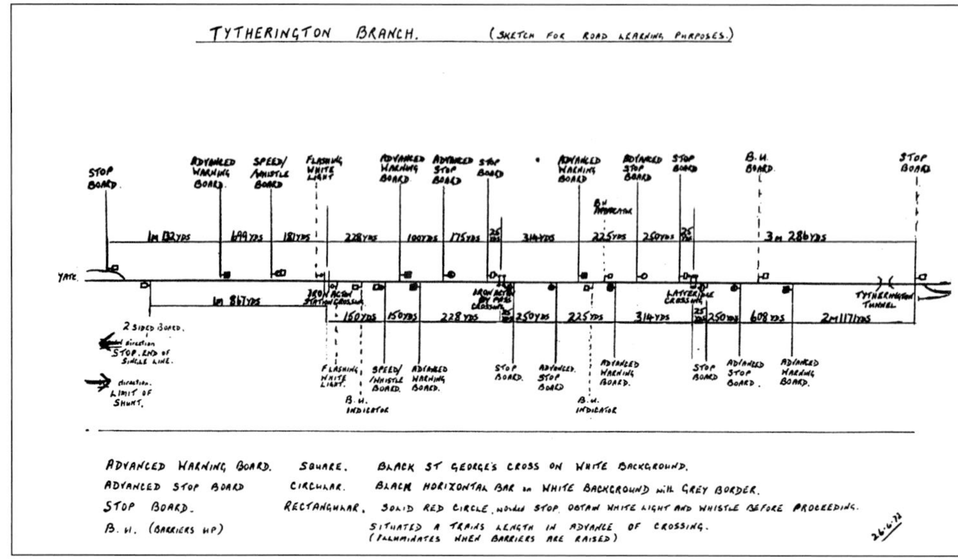

1972 signal sketches for route learning when the line re-opened from Yate to Tytherington Quarry.

Pressed Steel Co. No. W55034 motor brake second and driving trailer No. W56287 for use with single unit cars Nos. W55000-55035, at the Yate end of the Tytherington branch, 21st August, 1972. They were being used for driver training duty on the recently re-opened branch. *Author*

The well-built Iron Acton overbridge; warning cross for the by-pass crossing and rear of the speed restriction sign for Iron Acton crossing. View taken 10th April, 1991 when the line was out of use. *Author*

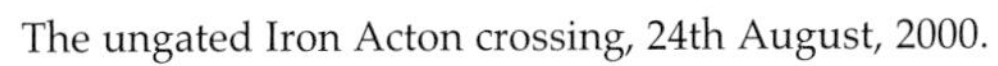

The ungated Iron Acton crossing, 24th August, 2000. *Author*

Latteridge crossing 10th April, 1991: barriers and the former crossing keeper's lodge. *Author*

Cattle grid at Latteridge crossing, 10th April, 1991. *Author*

terminates 8-10 ft above the original track level. The total cost of relaying the branch was approximately £140,000 of which ARC paid 40 per cent. The *Bristol Evening Post* of 1st August, 1972 said that people arrived late at work due to trains crossing the Iron Acton by-pass between 7.00 and 9.00 am and 5.00 and 6.00 pm. Rail movements were then prohibited from 7.45 to 8.30 am and 5.00 to 6.00 pm.

A grand official re-opening ceremony was performed by BR Chairman, Richard Marsh on 3rd September, 1973, 101 years and one day after the line had been first opened. It so chanced that 3rd September was the day when the 1,000th train ran over the re-opened line - at that time about four trains ran daily.

In the 1980s ARC spent £40m developing Whatley Quarry, near Frome, into the largest rail-connected aggregates quarry in the world. Then, with the coming of the 1990 trade recession, the rail connection at Tytherington was temporarily closed and all rail transported stone sent from Whatley, but later demand picked up and Tytherington was re-opened. Reserves at Tytherington will last for many years.

The official re-opening of the Tytherington branch, 3rd September, 1973. *Left to right*: Peter Edwards (ARC); Richard Marsh (BR Chairman); Stephen P.A. Savery (ARC) and F. Wright (General Manager, BR/WR). Behind Stephen Savery and F. Wright is a 'Western' class diesel-hydraulic hauling inspection saloon DW 975707. *Author's Collection*

The official re-opening ceremony at Tytherington Quarry, 3rd September, 1973. Stephen Savery area director, ARC, *left*; and F. Wright, General Manager BR/WR, *right*. *Author's Collection*

PGA type wagons being loaded at Tytherington Quarry *c.*1972. *Author's Collection*

Type '4' No. 1857 leaving Tytherington Quarry on 3rd July, 1972 with the first stone train after re-opening. *Author's Collection*

At Latteridge Crossing on 3rd July, 1972 Brush class '4' No. 1857 heads the first train from Tytherington Quarry after the branch had been re-opened. The advertisement on the former crossing cottage is for cabbage plants, etc. *Author's Collection*

Treadle to operate Iron Acton by-pass crossing barrier and lights, 10th April, 1991. *Author*

Brush type '4' No. 1857 on the Iron Acton by-pass crossing *en route* to Wolverton with the first train from Tytherington Quarry following the re-opening of the line on 3rd July, 1972.
Author's Collection

Type '4' locomotive No. 1610 with a train of hopper wagons being filled *c*.1972.
Author's Collection

The stockpile at Tytherington Quarry and type '4' No. 1940, September 1973.
Author's Collection

Type '4' 'Peak' class locomotive No. 192 with a stone train, passes the site of Iron Acton station *en route* to Yate, 14th September, 1963. View towards the new by-pass level crossing.
W.H. Harbor/Author's Collection

As above, but view to Iron Acton crossing. The roof of the crossing lodge can be seen above the hedge.
W.H. Harbor/Author's Collection

Chapter Four

The Passenger Train Services

The inaugural passenger train service on the branch provided just two trains daily, one in the morning and one in the evening, both connecting at Yate with trains on the main line. All trains carried the three classes of passengers. Local people, not unreasonably, were dissatisfied with this sparse service and pressed for a midday train to be run and from 17th September, 1872 the MR obliged. Trains were restricted to a maximum speed of 45 mph, stopped at all stations and took 30 minutes each way for the distance of 7½ miles. Traffic received a boost in 1885 when an outgoing tide caused a whale to become stranded on the bed of the River Severn at Littleton Pill. With ropes and steam traction engines, local inhabitants managed to heave it to the bank where in two weeks, over 40,000 people came to view it, many walking the four miles from the railway terminus at Thornbury.

By July 1886 the time table offered two mixed trains each way daily and an additional two on market day, the second Wednesday in the month. Trains stopped at all stations and now took 22 minutes each way. Mixed trains were allowed 27-30 minutes for the journey. The August 1887 service offered three trains each way and an additional one on the second Wednesday. Apart from the first train from Yate to Thornbury which was mixed, all took 22 minutes. In July 1914 four trains ran each way, the first and last being through to, or from, Bristol (Temple Meads), times taken on the branch varying from 15 to 21 minutes. July 1922 saw three trains each way, the first and last still through to, or from, Bristol, but with times of 19-22 minutes. The time table for the summer of 1939 was similar, with three each way taking 19-22 minutes, with an additional late train Saturdays-only, and a mid-afternoon train Thornbury to Yate on the second Wednesday. The final time table in 1944 offered three trains each way taking 19-22 minutes.

In 1941 Parnall's aircraft works was dispersed to various parts of south Gloucestershire, namely Wickwar, Charfield and Dursley. As there was no run-round loop at Wickwar but only a single crossover, a push-pull set was used to convey workers between Bristol and Wickwar. As hitherto the 4.50 pm Thornbury to Bristol had carried workers from Yate, the push-pull now duplicated its path and so the train originating from Thornbury terminated at Yate.

Passenger trains on the Thornbury branch usually comprised three coaches, but on Mondays and Fridays the set was strengthened with another two coaches. Passenger stock was stabled overnight at the passenger platform at Thornbury and cleaned by a porter. Vehicles over 57 ft in length and 9 ft 4 in. in width were prohibited from travelling over the line. At Thornbury the spring points were set to the run-round and coaches stored on the right-hand line north of the cattle dock. Due to wartime conditions requiring civilian train travel to be reduced, cheap day tickets were withdrawn on 5th October, 1942. Branch passenger trains were withdrawn from Monday 19th June, 1944, the last

Class '1P' 0-4-4T No. 1388 and train of four coaches at Thornbury *c.*1907. The paper boys' satchels are branded: *'Bristol Times & Mirror'*. *M.J. Tozer Collection*

The Oldown Troop at Thornbury station *c.*1914. Oldown is about 2 miles south-west of Thornbury. *M.J. Tozer Collection*

Another view of the Oldown Troop at Thornbury station *c.*1914. *M.J. Tozer Collection*

The Oldown Troop return to Thornbury *c.*1914, the horses having de-trained from the boxes. The advertisement for Millennium Flour shows forward thinking! *M.J. Tozer Collection*

YATE AND THORNBURY.

Miles.	For continuation of trains from junctions, see page		WEEKDAYS. 1	2	3	4	5	6	7	8	9	10	11	12	13	14	15
			PASSENGER (MIXED)				Empty Carriages.		PASSENGER (MIXED)		PASSENGER 6.20 p.m. from Bristol (T.M.).						PASSENGER
							A										SO
			a.m.				p.m.		p.m.		p.m.						p.m.
0	342 / 370	YATE ....dep.	9 58				2 0		3 30		6 57						9 58
2		Iron Acton..................	10 7				..		3 36		7 3						10 4
5¼		Tytherington	10 15						3 45		7 11						10 12
7½		THORNBURY ....arr.	10 20				2 15		3 51		7 16						10 17

Miles.	For continuation of trains from junctions, see page		WEEKDAYS. 1	2	3	4	5	6	7	8	9	10	11	12	13	14	15
			PASSENGER		PASSENGER				PASSENGER (MIXED)			PASSENGER (MIXED)					PASSENGER
									A								SO
			a.m.		a.m.				p.m.			p.m.					p.m.
0		THORNBURY ...dep.	7 48		10 32				2 30			4 50					9 18
2¼		Tytherington ...... arr.	7 53		10 37				2 36			4 55					9 23
		Tytherington ...... dep.	7 54		10 38				2 37			4 56					9 24
5½	342 / 370	Iron Acton..................	8 2		10 46				2 46			5 5					9 33
7½		YATE ....arr.	8 7		10 51				2 51			5 10					9 38

A—Runs on the Second Wednesday in each month.

Working timetables 1st May, 1939

Passenger timetable, 6th October, 1941

Table 267 YATE and THORNBURY

Miles from Yate		Week Days only a.m		p.m	p.m			
	Temple Meads 210Bristol .... dep	7‖50	..	1‖20	6 35	..	..	..
	210Bath (Queen Sq.) "	7 22	..	1222	5 42	..	..	..
	210Gloucester ..... "	7 45	..	1242	5 40	..	..	..
	Yate................ dep	9 10	..	4 5	7 15	..	..	..
2	Iron Acton...............	9 19	..	4 11	7 21	..	..	..
5¼	Tytherington............	9 27	..	4 20	7 29	..	.	..
7¾	Thornbury .... arr	9 32	..	4 26	7 34	..	..	..

Miles		Week Days only a.m	E	S		p.m		
	Thornbury .... dep	8 11	1040	11 30	..	4 40	..	..
2¼	Tytherington............	8 17	1046	11 36	..	4 46	..	..
5½	Iron Acton...............	8 25	1054	11 44	..	4 54	..	..
7½	Yate F............. arr	8 30	1059	11 49	..	4 59	..	..
34¼	210Gloucester ..... arr	10 47	2 46	1 11	..	6 49	..	..
22¾	210Bath (Queen Sq.) "	9 48	1 8	1 8	..	6 48	..	..
17¾	210Bristol (T.M.)... "	9§26	1228	12 28	..	5R52	..	..

§ Passengers can arr Bristol (St. Philips) 9 21 a.m. E Except Sats. F Station for Chipping Sodbury (1¾ miles).
R Bristol (St. Philip's). S Saturdays only. ‖ Passengers can dep Bristol (St. Philips) 8 20 a.m. and 1 14 p.m. respectively.

train actually running on this day. Parcels traffic to and from Tytherington and Thornbury was then conveyed by freight train. Except for coal traffic Iron Acton station was closed completely.

Bus competition had arrived on the scene early, from 5th February, 1906 Bristol Tramways Carriage Co. operating a service linking Thornbury with the tram terminus at Horfield Barracks. Several theories explained the withdrawal of passenger trains: one being the sparsity of passengers and another observing that at night the single line staff was at the wrong end of the branch if required for use by an ambulance train (*see below*). After withdrawal of the passenger service, goods trains sometimes unofficially carried passengers from Iron Acton or Tytherington. About 1958 one morning a lady arrived at Yate with a single ticket from Oswestry to Thornbury. The booking clerk at Oswestry had calculated the fare from the mileage, not realising that the passenger service had been withdrawn some 14 years previously. As the goods train to Thornbury had not yet left Yate, the station master arranged for her to ride in the brake van.

Branch passenger trains carried mail, the bags being transported on a hand cart between Thornbury station and the post office. It was not unusual for four to five baskets of pigeons to be dispatched by the local pigeon fanciers' club. One interesting item of parcels traffic was the occasional Severn salmon sent in a wicker basket carried on the shoulder to and from the railway van. At Tytherington in the 1890s, a village character, Ray Perry, watched where foxes were earthed for Squire Hardwicke's hunt, then crept out at night and killed them, sending their skins by train to a Bristol furrier.

In 1948-9 the Thornbury station master explained the decrease in parcels traffic and at that period it would have travelled on the zonal lorry, the 3 ton Dennis. In September 1948 there was a reduction in eggs arriving for the hatchery; in October and November less fruit trees were being sent from Forest & Orchard Nurseries, while December showed a reduction in radio parts from the manufacturers Messrs Aplin, Thornbury, to Messrs Murphy, while there were also fewer Christmas parcels dispatched. In February 1949 eggs were being sent to Flax Bourton by road rather than rail. July 1948 was the only month which brought better news - new traffic was vegetables from Messrs Howell sent to Birmingham.

Special passenger trains included Sunday school excursions, Weston-super-Mare being a popular destination. *Circa* 1943 a 12-coach train carrying United States' troops was taken from Bristol (Temple Meads) to Thornbury (where the soldiers were to be billeted), by two class '2P' 4-4-0s - one probably No. 520. It was a very dark night and as they had received an air raid warning, the footplate crews had secured the blackout sheets to prevent the possibility of firebox glow being seen by enemy aircraft. Because the driver of the pilot engine had signed for knowledge of the road to Thornbury, he changed locomotives and handled the train engine as the other driver was only fairly familiar with the branch, though events proved that the latter saved disaster from happening.

The single line staff was picked up at Yate and in due course the engines climbed through Tytherington, and beyond Grovesend tunnel galloped down towards Thornbury, the fireman on the leading engine peering out through the restricted view and seeing shells and bombs exploding at Bristol. The driver

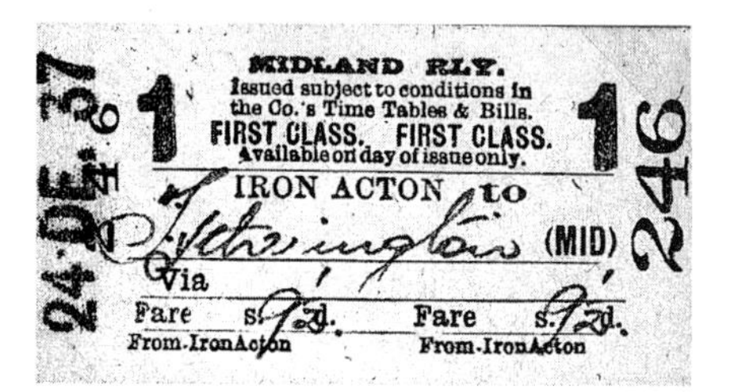

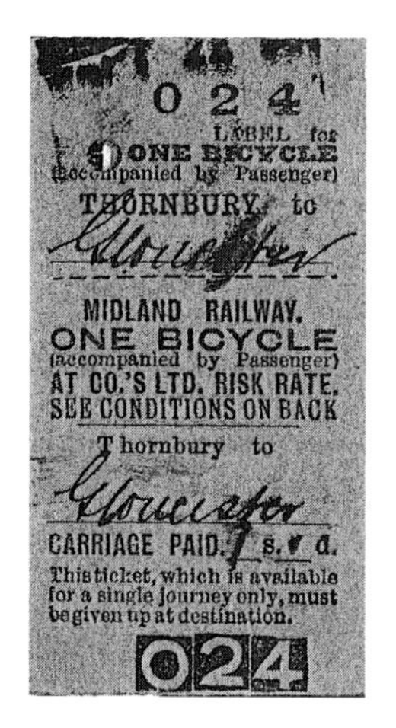

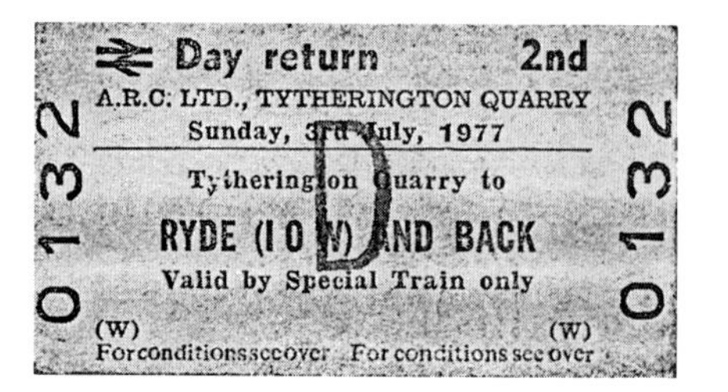

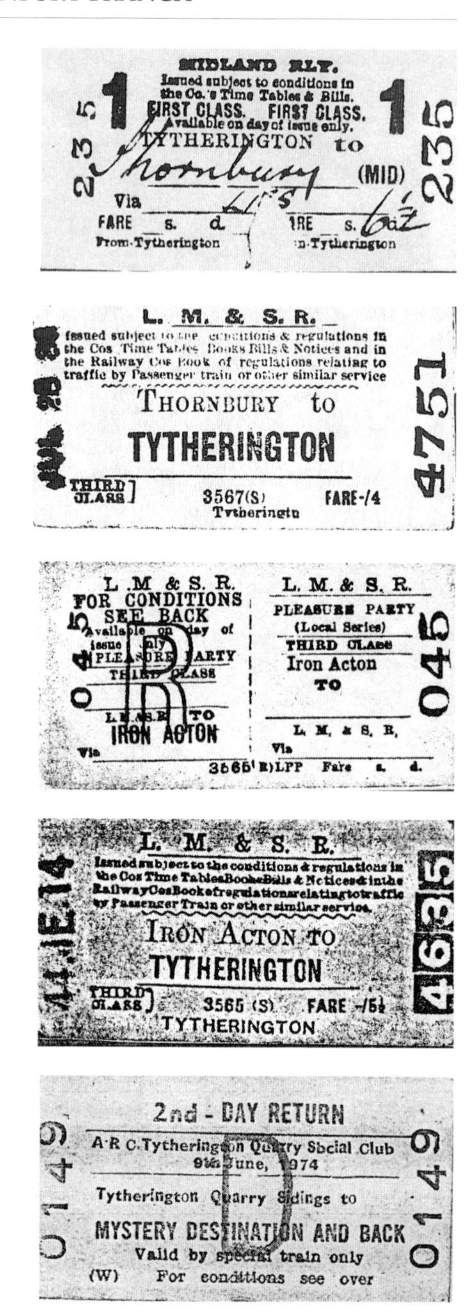

A selection of tickets used on the Thornbury line through the years.

came over to look at the raid for himself and suddenly exclaimed: 'Blimy! Goods shed!' and so saying violently applied the brakes. The train shuddered to a halt a mere tender's length from the blocks.

Other special traffic during World War II included ambulance trains carrying patients to the United States' Army Hospital at Leyhill, adjoining Tortworth Court, situated about five miles north-east of Thornbury. All the stone and building materials required for the hospital (now an open prison) were supplied by Grovesend Quarry. Although some ambulance trains had vacuum-braked coaches, the 10 used by the United States' army were Westinghouse-braked and so were required to be hauled by a London & North Eastern Railway (LNER), ex-Great Eastern Railway, 'B12/3' class 4-6-0 which had a permanent crew of two drivers, two firemen, a fitter and two guards who lived permanently on the train. With a Westinghouse-braked train the 'B12/3' had to be the train engine, but a vacuum-braked engine could assist in front. All the ambulance trains were in grey/khaki livery with white roofs, boldly displaying the Geneva Red Cross on roof and sides.

The ten 14-coach ambulance trains, numbered 11 to 15, 27, 31, 33, 36 and 37, consisted of a fixed rake of:

Car No.	
01	Brake third converted to brake/boiler/stores van
02 to 08	Corridor luggage van converted to ward car
09	Brake third corridor converted to brake/boiler/stores van
10/11	Sleeping car converted to staff car
12	Restaurant car converted to kitchen
13	Tourist saloon converted to sitting patients' car
14	Brake third corridor converted to brake/baggage/staff van

The first ambulance train arrived at Thornbury on 14th April, 1944 with 275 passengers, the 11 vacuum-braked coaches and luggage van headed by two class '3F' 0-6-0s. One of the Bristol engines had failed at Yate, so the Thornbury class '3F' (it may well have been No. 3712 which was shedded at Thornbury for a long time), had to be hastily dispatched to assist. The train arrived at the throat of Thornbury yard at 6.00 pm. The Bristol engine which was leading, was cut off at the point box (a covered ground frame), and run into the goods yard. The Thornbury engine drew the train into the platform at 6.09 pm. Eight coaches were at the platform, but the last three were for staff and the van for luggage, so not being at the platform was not a serious matter. The van was drawn off by the Bristol engine and placed in the yard for unloading. On departure of the empty stock, the Thornbury engine led.

The next ambulance train arrived on 10th June, 1944 from Sherborne. One engine came from Bath and the other from Thornbury. The 249 passengers did not have individual tickets, a warrant covered them all. The next ambulance train arrived on 14th June, 1944 from Wool, the 14-coach train piloted by the Thornbury engine. The following day a nine-coach ambulance train arrived at the Thornbury point box at 12.53 pm and reached the platform at 1.00 pm, but an error had been made and it was not destined for Thornbury, so left for an unrecorded destination at 1.56.

'16XX' class 0-6-0PT No. 1625 working the Railway Enthusiasts' Club's 'Severn Venturer' to Thornbury on 15th April, 1956, halts *en route* at Iron Acton. *Hugh Ballantyne*

'16XX' class 0-6-0PT No. 1625 at Tytherington station with the Railway Enthusiasts' Club's 'Severn Venturer' *en route* to Thornbury, 15th April, 1956. *Hugh Ballantyne*

The 21st June, 1944 saw the arrival of the first ambulance train following the withdrawal of the branch passenger service. The 14 Westinghouse-braked coaches from Wimborne were drawn over the Thornbury branch by an LNER 'B12/3' class engine with an LMS class '4F' 0-6-0 leading. It reached the point box at 3.15 pm. The class '4F' was taken to the turntable, the author of the Thornbury Daily Event Book commenting that this was 'an unwise move'. The LNER engine and the first seven coaches were then run into the 'Straight' - the run-round loop - at 3.25 pm. The LNER engine was then run forward, reversed along the platform road and drew the remaining seven coaches into the platform at 3.35. The LMS engine was now trapped on the turntable. The train was unloaded at 4.50 and then the kitchen car needed replenishing with water. The LNER engine pushed the coaches at the platform up the bank towards Grovesend tunnel and left them there. It then pushed those on the 'Straight' to the stop block. The LMS engine, now released, drew the coaches on the bank back to the platform. The LNER engine coupled to them and set back on to the rear portion on the straight. This did not allow clearance, as the LNER engine fouled the points at the station throat preventing the LMS engine from leaving the platform road. The LNER engine left tender-first at 6.15 pm with the LMS engine, banking at the rear. No warrant had been supplied for the passengers.

On 26th June, 1944 two LMS engines arrived with 11 coaches from Wool containing 136 cot and 125 walking cases. Stretchers were flat, but cots had sides and were used by patients who needed to be restrained. The first three coaches contained personnel for staffing the train. On 11th July, 1944 a train arrived with 223 stretcher and 68 sitting cases and no warrant was supplied. Steps were not used to assist unloading from coaches on the 'Straight'. The 26th July, 1944 saw 14 coaches arrive from Marlborough; again no warrant was offered. On 1st August, 1944 LMS and LNER engines arrived with 14 coaches containing 123 stretcher and 152 sitting cases. A drawbar was broken on LMS third class corridor coach No. 1302 and a spare inserted by the LNER fitter travelling on the train. No warrant was supplied for the passengers. On 15th August, 1944 a 13-coach Southern Railway ambulance train arrived with 126 cot and 169 sitting cases. The steps were not used for unloading. On 7th September, 1944 a 14-coach train arrived with 228 cot and 64 sitting cases. After unloading, the train returned to Westbury. On 19th September, 1944 another 14-coach train arrived, this time with 175 stretcher and 75 sitting cases. On 5th October, 1944 LMS engines brought in 11 coaches with 126 cot and 158 sitting cases. As the latter could be carried through the coaches to the platform, the train did not need to be split. No warrant was supplied. On 15th October, 1944, 14 coaches arrived behind an LNER and LMS engine. After unloading the 190 stretcher and 102 sitting cases, the train was ready to depart at 8.45 pm, but had to await the arrival of the fireman who had hurt his wrist and had to been taken to Leyhill for an X-ray. Again the train was not split, no steps were used and no warrant offered.

The person who made the entries in the Daily Event Book was on leave, and on his return, as no exact details were available, he simply recorded that ambulance trains arrived on two Sundays between 29th October and 18th November. On 22nd November, 1944, 180 stretcher and 30 sitting cases arrived

'16XX' class 0-6-0PT No. 1625 with the Railway Enthusiasts' Club's 'Severn Venturer' at Thornbury on 15th April, 1956. The first coach is 'Nondescript' brake third saloon No. 9103 (designed to accommodate parties). Built in May 1929 it is now preserved by the Severn Valley Railway. Its last use in BR service was in February 1961 on a special hauled by *City of Truro* to launch Westward Television. The water tower and engine shed, *right*, can be seen on the far right. *Author's Collection*

No. 1625 has run round its train, an enthusiasts' special organised by the RCTS, and is being watered at Thornbury on 26th September, 1959. *Dr A.J.G. Dickens*

in 11 coaches, the steps not being used. On 30th November, 1944 the 14 coaches held 278 cot cases, while an 11 coach train arrived on 8th December, 1944. On 26th December, 1944, 12 coaches arrived containing 180 cot and 30 sitting cases. The train's departure was delayed by having to fill the coach water tanks. This was made more difficult by the fact that the station tap was frozen and no hose pipe was available. The tap was eventually unfrozen and a pipe borrowed from a coal merchant. On 13th January, 1945, 240 cot and 30 sitting cases arrived and on 1st February, 1945 the final ambulance trains appeared, 137 cot and 150 sitting cases from Southampton. Just before the station throat, the leading engine was uncoupled and run forward into the loop. When the train engine attempted to 'ease up' to compress the buffers in order to uncouple, it lacked sufficient power to overcome the weight of the train on the 1 in 50 gradient and the first engine had to be brought back to assist. No warrant was available.

Following the line's re-opening for stone traffic, excursion trains starting from the quarry were run under the aegis of the ARC Tytherington Quarry Social Club.

Year		*Destination*
1974		Isle of Wight (advertised as a mystery tour)
1975		Newquay
1976		Southend
1977		Isle of Wight
1978		Brighton
1979		Weymouth
1980		Tenby
1981		Margate/Broadstairs/Ramsgate
1982	4th July	Isle of Wight
1982	22nd August	Isle of Wight
1983		Dawlish/Teignmouth/Torquay/Paignton
1984		Weymouth
1985		Eastbourne
1986		Dawlish/Teignmouth/Torquay/Paignton

For the first three trips a 3-car dmu was used carrying approximately 162 passengers. On 9th June, 1974 Gloucester Railway Carriage & Wagon Co. class '119' 'Cross-Country' unit B577 was utilised, passengers boarding via a small temporary platform. In 1977 and subsequently, so many employees wished to participate that a train of coaches hauled by a diesel engine was required to carry the 500 passengers. As the social club wished to run a bar on the first 3-car train, Thornbury magistrates were approached for a licence to open one on the Tytherington to Yate leg of the journey - what happened after that was apparently of no concern to the Thornbury magistrates. It is understood that in the following years a bar was opened and nothing was said. Two trips were made in 1982 because the organiser always allotted seats and wrote a seat number on every ticket. The wrong train was sent, seat numbers were different so some families could not sit together. As compensation, a free trip was arranged later that year.

Car No. 51091, *nearest*, of dmu set No. B577, under the stone loader at Tytherington Quarry prior to a mystery tour (to the Isle of Wight) for ARC employees and friends on 9th June, 1974.
Author's Collection

Car No. 51063, *right*, and No. 59422, *left*, of dmu set No. B577 at Tytherington Quarry with an employees' excursion to the Isle of Wight, 9th June, 1974. The luggage section of No. 51063 has been set up as a bar.
Author's Collection

Chapter Five

Goods and Mineral Traffic

The first traffic was iron ore from Frampton Cotterell which began in May 1870 before the line to Thornbury was completed. With the opening to Thornbury on 2nd September, 1872 wagon loads of grain formed one of the first trains. In the early years most of the trains were mixed (passenger and goods vehicles), the only separate working being a train taking empties from Yate to Tytherington and returning with loaded stone wagons. Certainly by 1914 it was a Bristol engine which worked this train, later in the day working the 11.15 am Yate to Thornbury and the 12.15 pm Thornbury to Yate, both mixed trains,the goods wagons being taken on to Westerleigh. The Thornbury engine worked the 1.15 pm Yate to Thornbury, the afternoon down and the 5.02 pm Thornbury to Bristol St Philip's service. In the summer of 1939 a separate mineral train was run allowing 20 minutes for shunting at Grovesend Quarry; 10 minutes at Tytherington and 10 minutes at Iron Acton. Additionally two mixed down and one mixed up trains were run. It is recorded that in 1940/41 tar arrived for the Tytherington Stone Co. and basic slag fertiliser for farmers, the latter product also at Tytherington in 1942/3.

In the summer of 1951 the branch was thriving to such an extent that an extra engine was required to work the daily service. The increased traffic largely consisted of ballast from the Tytherington Stone Co. and a large number of ex-GWR steel hopper wagons were branded 'Return to Tytherington'. These were superseded by new 20 ton capacity 'Herring' hopper wagons built in 1951 by Metro-Cammell, Nos. DB992197-992246.

From 1962 the branch was busy with traffic for building the Severn Bridge and the nuclear power station at Oldbury-on-Severn, both about four miles from Thornbury. Bulk cement arrived in 'Presflos' and steel came on bogie bolsters and in long wheelbase wagons. The steel was off-loaded by an 'Iron Fairy' crane and placed on one of about three 8-ton Thornycroft articulated lorries, a trailer being loaded while another was *en route*. Cement was taken to the construction site by R. & W. Febry & Sons, haulage contractors of Chipping Sodbury. Traffic was so heavy on the branch that the normal single weekdays-only working was augmented in 1964/65 by an additional trip on Tuesdays and Thursdays. This caused an unforeseen problem. The first train went over the branch early in the morning while it was still dark and on its first trip, ran though Iron Acton level crossing gates as they were unlit. During the first week the gates were run through on two occasions, so a lamp was fixed to them and also those at Latteridge. Road traffic was unused to finding gates across the road at such an early hour and there were some narrow misses with the closed gates.

Two sets of men were used. The second set booked on at Bristol, Bath Road at 11.23 am and caught a service bus to Yate and, relieved the early morning crew at about 1.00 pm, the latter returning to Bath Road by bus. The first trip took to Thornbury 'Presflos' and bogie bolsters for construction work, while the

YATE AND THORNBURY. (Single Line.)

STATIONS.	63 Passenger & Goods.	64 Passenger & Goods. A	65 Goods. E	66 Passenger & Goods. D	67 Passenger & Goods.
	a. m.	a. m.	noon	p. m.	p. m.
YATE ....dep.	9 43	11 30	12 0	2 26	5 45
Iron Acton	9 51	11 38	12 10	2 34	5 54
Tytherington	10 3	11 50	12 20	2 46	6 6
THORNBURY arr.	10 12	12 0	..	2 55	6 15

Miles.	STATIONS.	68 Passenger & Goods.	69 Passenger & Goods.	70 Goods. E	71 Passenger & Goods A B	72 Passenger & Goods. T
		a. m.	a. m.	p m.	p. m.	p. m.
..	THORNBURY dep.	8 40	10 30	..	1 0	4 50
2¼	Tytherington	8 48	10 39	12 40	1 8	4 59
5½	Iron Acton	8 58	10 49	12 50	1 18	5 9
7½	YATE..........arr.	9 7	11 0	1 0	1 27	5 20

A [illegible] Trains will run on the Second Wednesday in the Month. B--Works stone from Tytherington. D--Places empties in Stone Sidings, Tytherington, on the second Wednesday in each Month. E--Second Wednesday of each month excepted. T--Stops at New Siding, Tytherington.

Working timetable July 1886.

Working timetable July 1914.

YATE AND THORNBURY (SINGLE LINE)—WEEKDAYS.

Miles.	STATIONS.	1	2 See page 403. Empties. BX	3 Passenger 9.26 a.m. ex Bristol. D	4 Mixed. B	5	6	7 Mineral	8 Empties. B Q	9 Mixed.	10 Empties. Q	11	13 Passenger 6.18 p.m. ex Bristol. H	14
			a.m.	a.m.	a.m.			p.m.	p.m.	p.m.	p.m.		p.m.	
..	YATE .... dep.	.....	8 37	9 52	11 27	.....	.....	1 15	2 35	3 10	4 40	.....	6 45	.....
2	Iron Acton	..	..	9 56	11 33	..	..	1 30	2 40	3 16	..	..	6 49	..
5¼	Tytherington	.....	8 50	10 2	11 42	.....	.....	.....	.....	3 25	.....	.....	6 55	.....
7½	THORNBURY arr.	..	..	10 7	11 48	..	..	2 0	..	3 31	4 55	..	7 0	..

Miles.	STATIONS.	1	2 See page 382. Passenger to Bristol.	3 Mineral. B	4 Passenger	5	6	7	8 See page 389. Mineral to Westerleigh. B	9 Passenger E	10 Mineral. B Q	11 Mineral. Q	12 Mixed to Bristol. S.P. 390.	13
			a.m.	a.m.	a.m.				p.m.	p.m.	p.m.	p.m.	p.m.	
..	THORNBURYdep	.....	8 12	...	10 47	.....	.....	.....	12 15	2 12	.....	3 50	5 2	.....
2¼	Tytherington	..	8A20	9 35	10 53	..	..	..	12 50	2 19	..	4 20	5 9	..
5½	Iron Acton	.....	8 26	.....	10 59	.....	.....	.....	1 5	2 28	2 50	.....	5 18	.....
7½	YATE.........arr.	..	8 30	9 50	11 3	..	..	..	1 14	2 33	3 0	4 35	5 23	..

A—Arrives at Tytherington at 8.17 a.m. B—Bristol engine works these trips. All other trains worked by Thornbury engine. D—See page 415. E—Runs as "Mixed" train on the second Wednesday in each month. H—See page 413. X—Does not exceed 34 wagons from Yate.

second train took other traffic such as coal, general goods, farm implements to Thornbury and coal to various sidings and empty wagons to Tytherington Quarry. Wagons for the second train had been taken from Westerleigh to Yate by the Charfield 'tripper'. The cement and steel for the first train had been dropped off at Yate by a down freight. These two products made a heavy load, so a class '4F' would charge up to the tunnel from Tytherington station with its train dropping sand in an attempt to overcome dampness and leaf problems in the cutting, with trees brushing the sides of the engine. On days when only one train ran, the engine ran light to Westerleigh and left there about 10.00 am, arriving at Thornbury for lunch. Due to the steep gradient, the loading for a class '4F' was 24 mineral wagons, but on 4th April, 1962 0-6-0 diesel-electric shunter No. D4022 successfully worked a load equal to 25 mineral wagons.

Celestine (strontium sulphate) was manually mined by the open-cast method in the area on the site now occupied by Yate Shopping Centre. The mineral was used for sugar beet refining, ceramics, purifying caustic soda and for use in the paint and steel industries. Because it burns with a bright red flame, it is useful for fireworks, distress and signal flares and tracer shells. In 1939 Yate produced 95 per cent of the world's supply and, until mining ceased *circa* 1950, this was dispatched from Yate and Chipping Sodbury stations. It was stacked in the station yard and when an appreciable amount had been accumulated, trucks were ordered.

Parnall's site at Yate had been used for constructing aircraft during World War I, the Royal Flying Corps operating from an adjacent flying field. Abandoned after the cessation of hostilities, George Parnall & Co. took over the factory buildings in 1925. Ten years later a new undertaking was set up - Parnall Aircraft Ltd which built Fraser-Nash aircraft turrets. In addition to this work the firm also became the largest sub-contractor in the country for making 'Spitfire' components.

Messrs Newman's factory also started during World War I and produced aero engines. During World War II it made shells and these were loaded on to railway wagons. Both factories were the target of a daylight attack by enemy raiders on 28th February, 1942 when heavy casualties were sustained. In the 1950s Newman's built electric motors for driving machinery, while Parnall (Yate) Ltd manufactured washing machines, wringers and cookers.

The Fishponds Coal Co. had a depot at Yate dealing with domestic sales, while Messrs Lowell Baldwin, supplied Newman Industries' factory from the station yard. In the 1950s stock feed potatoes, dyed blue so as not to be used for human consumption, arrived at Yate for farms in the district. In season, seed potatoes would be received from Scotland in vans, the load often sheeted inside the van to protect it from frost damage. Another inwards traffic for farmers was bags of basic slag. Relief porters were sent from Temple Meads when supplies arrived for Ford & Cannings' buffer depot across the road. Consumables included soya beans, boxes of dried fruit, maize starch and sacks of cattle food from Avonmouth. Some of these supplies were distributed locally, while others left by rail.

About 1952 when British Road Services' lorries were auctioned at Westerleigh, some destined for Ireland travelled by rail from Yate as they were unroadworthy. By the 1950s, although a livestock market was held adjacent to the station, the cattle dock was little used, the last occasion being *circa* 1960 to

THORNBURY AND YATE.

Miles.	For continuation of trains from junctions see page		WEEKDAYS. 1	2 Engine & Brake.	3 Mineral.	4	5 Mineral.	6
				SUSPENDED. SO a.m.	✻ p.m.		SUSPENDED. SO ✻ p.m.	
0		THORNBURY .... ♀...dep.	..	9 35	1 0	..	2 25	..
1		Grovesend	..	..	1 30	..	2 40	..
2¼		Tytherington	..	..	1 45	..	..	..
5½		Iron Acton	..	..	2 7	..	..	..
7½	682	YATE .... ♀...arr.	..	9 50	2 17	..	3 5	..

3.—Arrives Grovesend 1.10, Tytherington 1.35, Iron Acton 1.57. On Second Wednesday in each month leaves Thornbury 12.50 p.m., Grovesend arr. 1.0 p.m., dep. 1.15, Iron Acton arr. 1.30, dep. 1.40, Yate arr. 1.47.
5.—E. & B. to Grovesend, arr. 2.30.

Miles.	For continuation of trains from junctions see page		WEEKDAYS. 1 Empties.	2	3 Empties.	4	5 Engine & Brake.	6
			SUSPENDED. SO ✻ a.m.		✻ a.m.		SUSPENDED. SO p.m.	
0	687	YATE .... ♀....dep.	8 40	..	11 45	..	1 45	..
2		Iron Acton	..	..	..	..	..	..
5¼		Tytherington	..	..	..	..	..	..
6½		Grovesend	9 15	..	12 20	..	..	..
7½		THORNBURY .... ♀....arr.	9 25	..	12 30	..	2 0	..

1.—Grovesend arr. 9.10.
3.—Grovesend arr. 12.6.

Working timetable 1st May-24th September, 1939.

Working timetable September 1953.

THORNBURY AND YATE.

Miles.	Classification ..	WEEKDAYS.			J			
	Target No. ..				38			
					p.m.			
0	THORNBURY .... ♀...dep.	..	..	..	3 30	..	..	..
1	Grovesend .... arr.	..	..	..	3 40	..	..	..
	dep.	..	..	..	3 55	..	..	..
2¼	Tytherington .... arr.	..	..	..	4 5	..	..	..
	dep.	..	..	..	4 15	..	..	..
5½	Iron Acton .... arr	..	..	..	4 30	..	..	..
	dep	..	..	..	4 40	..	..	..
7½	YATE .... ♀...arr.	..	..	..	4 50	..	..	..

Miles.	Classification ..	WEEKDAYS.			J			
	Target No. ..				38			
					p.m.			
0	YATE .... ♀....dep.	..	..	..	1 35	..	..	..
2	Iron Acton .... arr.	..	..	..	..	..	..	..
	dep.	..	..	..	..	..	..	..
5¼	Tytherington .... arr.	..	..	..	..	..	..	..
	dep.	..	..	..	..	..	..	..
6½	Grovesend .... arr.	..	..	..	2 5	..	..	..
	dep.	..	..	..	2 15	..	..	..
7½	THORNBURY .... ♀....arr.	..	..	..	2 30	..	..	..

convey sheep during a foot and mouth disease epidemic as rail transport was the only permitted method to move uninfected livestock out of a restricted area.

About 1964 during the early days of the Yate Industrial Estate adjoining the station, Everlasting Construction Co., which received steel from Teeside, often dispatched the finished product by road, much to the disappointment of the railway salesman. In an effort to prevent the road operator receiving a return load to Birmingham, the company was offered a very low flat rate of £5 for a bogie bolster wagon Yate to Birmingham, the railway also providing for this sum, collection and delivery. The offer was accepted and although it was probably uneconomic for BR, at least the road operator had to forgo his return load. Also *circa* 1964 Messrs Alvan Blanche manufactured agricultural machinery at Yate, the finished product being loaded on continental wagons for destinations in Hungary.

Yate goods shed had a Midland Railway 2 ton capacity lifting crane; *circa* 1952 it required repairs which the WR decided would not be practicable, so condemned it, the replacement being a redundant 30 cwt crane from St Agnes, Cornwall. It arrived in a wagon and was assembled by men from the Outdoor Machinery Department. Outside in the goods yard was a 5 ton Cowans-Sheldon hand crane with two gears. One day porters found it unusually hard work unloading a steel wagon and found they were lifting the wagon as well as its load!

The goods foreman's office and mess room were in one long building. The latter had an LMS range and two large LMS kettles always full of hot water. When a down freight stopped to set back into the Aircraft siding, its fireman usually jumped off his engine and ran over with a can to fetch hot water for tea.

At the north end of the goods yard near the entrance, was a weigh house with a 20 ton capacity weighing machine, latterly one manufactured in 1940 by H. Pooley & Sons Ltd. The weigh bridge was maintained by its makers, an ex-MR van branded 'Shunt with Care' periodically arriving with measuring equipment and weights. A Tilley lamp illuminated the weigh bridge house which was heated by a coal fire set in an iron grate with a stone and brick surround. A high desk ran the entire length of the office and was equipped with a suitably high stool.

The weigh house was unlocked every morning by a key about four inches in length and kept overnight in the station, as it was too large for a coat pocket. Each morning before weighing, any water had to be swept off, the machine balanced and an entry recording this fact recorded in the weighing book, noting date, time of day and signature. The weigh bridge was balanced by inserting a long, flat key into the pointed end of a long balancing bar. During the day the weigh bridge would be swept as often as necessary according to heavy rainfall, snow or falling coal.

A railway lorry was always weighed when it entered the yard with a load, even if the sender had declared a weight on the consignment note it had to be checked for accuracy. If the difference was only marginal, the railway let the sender's declared weight stand, otherwise it was corrected. Before leaving the yard to make a delivery, the railway lorry driver drew on to the weigh bridge for the load to be weighed and entered on a delivery sheet prepared for the consignee to sign that the delivery was correct.

L.M.S.
To ......GOODS AGENT,.................
Thornbury
(Centre No. 54)

From Chief Commercial Manager's Office,
WATFORD, H.Q.
F1/48450/33.
Ext. 347. 24th October, 1941.
Emergency Circular 35.

E.R.O. 34868.

EMERGENCY ROUTES FOR GOODS, MINERAL (EXCEPT COAL AND COKE) AND LIVE STOCK TRAFFIC.

Referring to L.M.S/L.N.E. Route Book dated 1st July 1937.

Will you please note that during the National Emergency until further advised, traffic for L.N.E. stations with route numbers 192, 193, 194, 197, 197A, 198 must be forwarded by the Routes as given below.

This instruction is to be placed in the back of your L.M.S/L.N.E. Route Book and the sign ϕ 24/10/41 inserted against the route numbers given above on page 17. It must be clearly understood by all concerned that where the sign ϕ 24/10/41 appears the Emergency Instruction of date named supersedes the present recorded route. No other alteration is to be made in the Route Book.

Route No.	Route
192	VIA LEEDS (NEVILLE HILL)
193	VIA NORMANTON except Cattal, Marston Moor, Hammerton, Pilmoor, Hessay, Poppleton — VIA LEEDS (ARMLEY) (Ammended)
194	VIA CUDWORTH
~~197~~	~~VIA CUDWORTH~~
~~197A~~	~~VIA CUDWORTH~~
~~198~~	~~VIA CUDWORTH~~

To operate on and from 27th October, 1941.

Please acknowledge receipt of this order to your District Goods Manager.

a.n. 27/10/41

T. E. ARGILE,
Chief Commercial Manager.

Letter to Thornbury goods agent re emergency routes.

Letter to the Yate station master dated 3rd July, 1943.

E.R.O. 24153

LMS INTERNAL CORRESPONDENCE

To

Mr. Lanham.
YATE. LMS. 54.
(Centre No.)

Our Reference: A1/14153
Your Reference

From DISTRICT GOODS & PASSENGER MANAGER'S OFFICE,
BRISTOL
EXTN. (Centre No. 55).

3rd July. 43.

Consigning of Goods "Carriage Paid" Maize Starch Distributors Association Ltd. 20 Stratford Place. W.1.

The Transport Manager of the above Association has complained that your people have declined to accept a consignment note made out shewing their name as senders for a consignment forwarded from Yate.

It has now been agreed following representations made by the Ministry of Food that Maize Starch should be treated as " Buffer Depot traffic" and the above Association have consignment notes made out in their name with an endorsement " Ex Buffer Depot", carriage charges payable by consignees.

p.t.o.

Class '4F' 0-6-0 No 44424 ascending the gradient of 1 in 61 to Grovesend tunnel on 22nd August, 1956. The tower of' Thornbury church can be seen above the trees towards the top right-hand corner. *Author*

Thornbury 1961, 'Presflos' galore: behind class '4F' 0-6-0 No. 44553 of 22A (Bristol, Barrow Road) and in sidings on each side. The cement used for the Severn Bridge and Oldbury-on-Severn power station construction set in 20 minutes. *Colin Roberts*

On 18th April, 1952 driver John Harford Richmond rests on his 6 ton Scammell mechanical horse, registration BNK 187, built in 1936. He had moved to Yate on promotion from a horse dray man at Bristol (St Philip's). Notice the starting handle by his left hand. The single head lamp left much to be desired on unlit country roads. Messrs Parnall (Yate) Ltd's factory is in the background. *Colin Roberts*

Dennis lorry, registration BNK 730, fleet No. 3927W seen in Yate station approach, 2nd July, 1953. The figure '3' in the fleet number denotes the vehicle's carrying capacity of 3 tons. Driver Stan Morse had been delivering beer to the Sheperdine and Oldbury-on-Severn areas which only received deliveries twice weekly, whereas those to Thornbury, Alveston and Tytherington were made daily. *Colin Roberts*

For public weighing, such as when metal was brought in from Parnall (Yate) Ltd, or Newman Industries Ltd for loading, a charge per ton rate was made and if not proceeding onwards by rail, was charged double rate. The Fishponds Coal Co. weighed bulk deliveries of coal and coke; Messrs Spackman, Staple Hill, weighed hay and straw. Spackman was generous and remembered for always giving a tip to the operator. Cohen of the 600 Group weighed scrap when the Bristol Brabazon aircraft was dismantled. The method for weighing a 12-wheel rigid wheelbase lorry which overlapped the weigh bridge, was to weigh the front portion first, the driver then moving forward to place the rear wheels on the machine and thus determine the total tare, or laden weight.

Two railway lorry drivers were based at Yate: Stanley Walter Morse was normally in charge of the 3 ton Dennis and John Harford Richmond, and later Bill Green, the 6 ton Scammell mechanical horse. Stanley commenced railway service on the MR in 1916 and always wore the leather gaiters issued to him previously to protect his legs in the days when lorry cabs were very sparse and draughty. His father had worked on the construction of the Thornbury branch. The Dennis arrived in 1946 when zonal collection and delivery for consignments up to one ton started from Yate on 12th August, 1946. It ran as far as Oldbury-on-Severn, Shepperdine and Oldbury Naite. The Dennis was withdrawn in the mid-1950s when the law required two rear reflectors to be fitted and BR did not believe it worthwhile to go to the expense of fitting them to this vehicle. In cold weather it did not readily start and the procedure was to remove the sparking plugs and warm them by the fire. No anti-freeze was used, so the radiator had to be drained when a night frost was anticipated. The Dennis's replacement was an Austin diesel Loadstar 2 ton lorry covered by a tarpaulin supported on hoops. Fuel for this vehicle was obtained from R. & W. Febry, haulage contractor at Chipping Sodbury. When diesel oil became scarce during the 1956 Suez crisis, he refused to supply and the Austin was temporarily replaced by a petrol-engined vehicle. Petrol posed no problem as in the early 1950s, due to an increase in the traffic carried, it was decided to install a 500 gallon petrol tank and hand pump by the rear of the down side of the passenger station. The railway lorries were left outside the passenger station overnight and the local population could be trusted - no keys were required to start the engine of the Scammell, merely turning a switch sufficed. The same procedure applied to replacement Thornycrofts.

Yate goods yard wheelbarrow, used for various jobs, was branded 'Tytherington' having been brought to Yate for further use when that station closed. It was of timber construction, the wooden wheel having a metal tyre. Yate closed to goods traffic on 20th June, 1966.

Iron Acton, which had a siding facing down trains, was normally worked by an up train, but the Working Time Table Appendix for March 1937 ruled that up to five vehicles, excluding a brake van, may be propelled from Yate to Iron Acton. Both Bristol Co-op and Thomas Silvey had a coal depot at Iron Acton. Latterly the coal merchants were the Co-op and Mr Gale who sold his business to his nephew Les Gale and also to John Eaves. At Tytherington, Arthur Skuse was the local coal merchant, his sister sharing the business and helping him carry the coal.

Class '4F' 0-6-0 No. 44296 awaits departure from Thornbury with a cement 'Presflo' and mineral wagon. It will collect loaded ballast wagons at Grovesend Quarry, September 1963.

W.F. Grainger

'Sam' E.H. Collins, the Thornbury porter and Caradoc Williams, Yate station master, by a brake van at Thornbury station, 17th August, 1956.

Author

In post-World War II years, goods trains on the branch travelling towards Thornbury mainly consisted of 6 to 12 coal wagons daily and empty ballast wagons. Emerging from Tytherington tunnel the guard dropped the brakes on the coal wagons, unhooked and allowed the engine to go forward with the empty ballast wagons, before reversing them into the loop where they could gravitate as required under the loading plant. The engine then coupled on to the rest of the train and took it down to Thornbury where the guard applied his brake hard, the engine uncoupled and ran to the water tower where a shunting pole was used to increase the leverage to pull down the chain. The engine was then turned, though some crews preferred to turn the engine before watering, as it was then lighter and, thus easier to push round. The balanced turntable could take nothing bigger than a class '4F' 0-6-0. Engines were not always turned, particularly if a driver was in a hurry.

If there were only a few wagons on the brake van, while the engine was being turned, the guard released his brake and the train gravitated slowly into the passenger platform. The watered engine would go over to the platform road, drop down on to the van and couple up. Having done this, the meal break was usually taken. After the crew had taken refreshment, the loaded coal wagons were shunted off and empties placed on the brake van standing at the platform. The train was remarshalled so that wagons for Tytherington and Iron Acton were next to the engine. If they had a short train, some crews stopped and picked water cress on the left hand side of the line before reaching Grovesend tunnel. It was not wise to do this with a long train as they might have experienced difficulties starting up the bank.

Point to point times for freight trains June 1953

Class of Freight	H *Passing allowance mins*	J, K *Passing allowance mins*	E, F, H, J, K *Standing allowance mins*	E, F, H, J, K *Stopping allowance mins*
Yate-Iron Acton	6	8	3	2
Iron Acton-Tytherington	9	10	3	2
Tytherington-Thornbury	8	10	3	2
Thornbury-Tytherington	9	10	3	2
Tytherington-Iron Acton	8	10	3	2
Iron Acton-Yate	6	8	3	2

Inwards traffic to Thornbury was principally coal for the Thornbury Coal Co. (formerly E.G. Watts) which had its own wagons, and A.J. Davis. If the town's fire alarm sounded when the men were busy unloading a wagon, one part-time fireman dropped his shovel, sprinted to the fire station and drove the fire engine. Other members of the crew included the local butcher. Thornbury Gas Works received four to five wagons of coal weekly, Pearce, the local haulier, using a horse and cart to carry the coal from the station to the works. Other items received at Yate were animal foodstuffs, fertiliser, farm machinery, sugar beet pulp - some in sacks and some loose in a wagon; Worthington and draught Bass for the Ship Hotel, Alveston and the Mason's Arms, Rudgeway. During World War II boxes of cordite were carried in fitted vans to Thornbury where it was stored in the disused Cox's brick works at Littleton-upon-Severn.

WEEKDAYS — YATE AND THORNBURY

DOWN

Mileage M	Mileage C			K		K	
				9F38		9F38	
				SO		SX	
				am		PM	
0	0	**YATE**	dep	10 5		1 0	
2	1	Iron Acton	arr	..	..	..	..
			dep				
5	22	Tytherington	arr	..	..	..	..
			dep				
5	67	Grovesend	arr	10 35	..	1 30	..
			dep	10 45		1 40	
7	43	**THORNBURY**	arr	11 0	..	1 55	..

UP

Mileage M	Mileage C			K		K	
				9F38		9F38	
				SO		SX	
				am		PM	
0	0	**THORNBURY**	dep	11 30		2 35	
1	56	Grovesend	arr	11 40	..	2 45	..
			dep	11 55		3 20	
2	21	Tytherington	arr	..	..	3 30	..
			dep			3 40	
5	42	Iron Acton	arr	..	..	3 55	..
			dep			4 5	
7	43	**YATE**	arr	12 30	..	4 15	..

Above: Working Timetable 12th June-10th September, 1961.

Below and right: Extract from Working Timetable 9th September, 1963-14th June, 1964.

Local Trip Working

BRISTOL 809

Ex LM. Class 4 (0-6-0)

Enginemen

Barrow Road

809A on duty 4.55 a.m. off duty 11.10 p.m. **SX**

	arr.	dep.	
	a.m.	a.m.	
Barrow Road Shed		5‖10	LE MO
Westerleigh Sidings	5‖30		
Barrow Road Shed		5‖10	LE MSX
Bristol (St. Philips)	5‖15	5†25	EBV
Westerleigh Sidings	5†45	6.15	TTHSX 9F32
Yate	6.30	8.6	
Rangeworthy	8.15	8.16	
Charfield	8.30	10.40	
Westerleigh Sidings	11.15		
	a.m.	a.m.	
Westerleigh Sidings	5†45	6.15	TTHO 9F38
Yate	6.30	8.0	
Grovesend	8.30	8.40	
Thornbury	8.55	9.40	
Grovesend	9.50	10.5	
Yate	10.40	11.0	
Westerleigh Sidings	11.15		
	p.m.	p.m.	
Westerleigh Sidings		12.5	SX 7B43
Fishponds	12.25	12†40	EBV 0F32
Bristol (St. Philips)	12†50	12‖55	LE
Barrow Road Shed	1‖0		

Local Trip Working

BRISTOL 810

Ex LM. Class 4 (0-6-0)

Enginemen

Barrow Road

810A on duty 9.0 a.m. off duty 6.0 p.m. **SX**
810A on duty 6.35 a.m. off duty 2.35 p.m. **SO**
810B on duty 3.45 p.m. off duty 11.45 p.m. **SX**
810B on duty 3.15 p.m. off duty 11.15 p.m. **SO**
810C on duty 10.20 p.m. D, off duty 6.20 a.m. **MX & SUN**

	arr.	dep.	
	a.m.	a.m.	
Barrow Road Shed		9‖15	LE SX
Yate	9‖35		
Shunt as required			
	p.m.	p.m.	
Yate		1.0	9F38
Grovesend	1 30	1.40	
Thornbury	1.55	2.35	9F38
Grovesend	2 45	3.20	
Yate	3 55		
Shunt as required			
Yate		6.30	SX
Westerleigh Sidings	6.43	7.20	9F38
Bristol (TM)	8	8	
West Depot	8 15	9.52	9F38
Pylle Hill	10.2	R10.20	
Westerleigh Sidings	11.5		
	a.m.	a.m.	
Westerleigh Sidings		2.5	MX 9F38
West Depot	3.0	3†10	EBV
Westerleigh Sidings	4†0	4.55	Q 6F38
Bristol (St. Philips)	5.28	5‖33	LE
Barrow Road Shed	5‖38		
	a.m.	a.m.	
Barrow Road Shed		6‖50	SO LE 0F35
Westerleigh Sidings	7‖25	7.30	9F38
Yate	7.46		
Shunt as required			
Yate		10.5	
Grovesend	10.35	10.45	
Thornbury	11.0	11 30	
Grovesend	11.40	11.55	
	p.m.	p.m.	
Yate	12.30	1‖0	LE
Barrow Road Shed	2‖0	4‖15	LE
Bristol (St. Philips)	4‖20	4.50	(Assist.)
Westerleigh Sidings	5.15		
Shunt			
Westerleigh Sidings		7.30	9F38 SO
West Depot	8.30	9.52	
Pylle Hill	10.2	R10.22	
Westerleigh Sidings	11.5		
	a.m.	a.m.	
Westerleigh Sidings		3.0	SUN 9F38
West Depot	4.15	5.10	
Bristol (T.M.)	5	22	
Bristol (St. Philips)	5.35	5‖40	LE
Barrow Road Shed	5‖45		

Traffic from Thornbury was generally light. Mr Grace, a relative of the cricketer, owned a saw mill at Thornbury and made seed boxes and railway sleepers, the latter for the LMS, and these were forwarded by rail. On the second Wednesday in the month when a cattle market was held at Thornbury, up to a dozen cattle vans would be taken to Bristol. Sugar beet brought in by farmers was loaded at the cattle dock and sent to Kidderminster, the quantities being:

Year	*Tonnage*	*Number of wagons*
1943-4	?	21
1944-5	?	18
1945-6	?	18
1946-7	79	11
1947-8	97	21
1948-9	190	?
1949-50	158	?

Loose lifting tackle at Thornbury comprised a pair of wool hooks of 10 cwt lifting capacity; a 1 ton double chain grab and two rope slings.

In the 1960s Mr Blann who owned a woodworking business at Thornbury, purchased a condemned 'A' container and this duly arrived on a 'one journey only' condemned GWR 'Conflat' wagon. The container was delivered to its purchaser who immediately filled it with export goods for Canada via the Victoria & Albert Docks. Thornbury goods department, not having another container flat available, placed it on the condemned wagon. At Westerleigh Yard the flat wagon was inspected and certified for a further journey.

In 1966 pipes were sent from Stanton Gate, Derbyshire to Thornbury for taking water from Purton, on the Gloucester & Berkeley Canal, to Littleton-upon-Severn treatment works. Delivery from Thornbury to Littleton was by railway lorry. Some of these pipes, which consignment had been canvassed to rail by the Divisional Office salesman, arrived labelled to Thornbury after the branch had closed (20th June), and so had to be re-labelled to Bristol and a great many extra road miles run.

Quarry Traffic

Quarry traffic brought a considerable income to the branch, and indeed today produces the only traffic. *Circa* 1883 Howell Lloyd Hardwicke, trading as the Tytherington Stone Co., wrote the following letter to Sir John Noble, the Midland Railway's General Manager:

Sir,

I have now got the working of the Tytherington stone quarries and anticipate doing a large business in stone.

I want a short branch line made into the quarries off the main line. I shall have much pleasure in laying down the branch line at my own expense and subject to the approval of your surveyor if you will allow me.

I shall be glad if you will give me a special rate for the carriage of stone an your line. I will guarantee you 6,000 tons of stone per annum on your line from my quarries.

H.L. Hardwicke

The plant at Grovesend Quarry *c.*1918. Italian prisoner-of-war huts can be seen on the left. At that period, POWs worked in the quarry. A hot tar hopper can be seen and wagons used by the Gloucestershire County Council. The steam lorry is owned by Rogers - grandfather of the present fairground machine owner.

Author's Collection

The result of this communication was a Private Siding Agreement dated 22nd October, 1884 allowing him to lay a siding to West Quarry. This standard gauge siding replaced a narrow gauge tramway which hitherto had brought stone to the MR's siding. A second standard gauge siding to West Quarry was added under a Private Siding Agreement of 28th February, 1895. The quarry was eventually taken over by Roads Reconstruction (1934) Ltd and a Private Siding Agreement made on 16th May, 1953. Hardwicke also owned Church Quarry on the opposite side of the line and a Private Siding Agreement was made for this on 22nd June, 1898. This quarry was also taken over by Roads Reconstruction and a Siding Agreement made with that company on 6th August, 1936. This Siding Agreement was terminated *circa* 1944.

On 4th June, 1885 a call came for the opinion of H.D. Greene QC in a dispute between the MR and Hardwicke's quarries, Tytherington. Hardwicke had inherited an estate in 1880 and, until the spring of 1885, was in complete ignorance of having any mineral rights within the limits of the MR's purchase of land for construction of the line. Since 1880 the MR had been carrying out extensive quarrying of stone at Tytherington and had a cutting to a depth of 40 ft removing 19,110 tons from Hardwicke's estate and 1,570 tons from land purchased from the Reverend C.W. Fox. The stone was of varying qualities - some loose and friable, other hard and suitable for building. The stone taken by the MR had been used at stations for making approaches, repairing roads, and occasionally for building. The MR admitted that there was no express mention of mines and minerals in the parcels of land conveyed to it. Hardwicke claimed that the railway company had no right to the minerals except for removal to build its line. The MR declined to pay Hardwicke any compensation alleging that:

1. Hardwicke had no right to work his minerals on its land and could therefore only obtain nominal damages.
2. That it had a right to quarry all stone included in its boundary down to formation level.
3. That it had the right to remove stone dislodged by landslip however caused, including judicious increase by artificial means.

Green was of the opinion that the MR was wrong in each of these contentions.

J.P. Sturge & Sons, surveyors, Bristol, made a report on 23rd June, 1885 and advised that Hardwicke's remedy would be to recover the value of the stone taken and bring action for damages. Judging from stone lying on the ground, Sturge said:

> The stone itself is of very good quality for building and some of it has been worked into large blocks and coping stones suitable for bridges and other railway works. Stone of this description with siding communication, to a Railway is worth a royalty of 4*d*. per ton, which on 20,680 amounts to £344 13*s*. 4*d*. If Hardwicke brought an action for the recovery of this amount, the company might allege that stone in this situation is not worth a royalty of 4*d*. per ton because Mr Hardwicke had no right to convey it over the MR line except by constructing and working a siding which would cost nearly, if not quite, the value of the stone.
>
> Hardwicke sends 100 tons of stone per day, say 30,000 tons per annum at average railway carriage rate of 2*s*. 3*d*. per ton equal to £3,375 per annum. Having the entire control of his traffic, the MR are in a position to charge the maximum legal rates and if Hardwicke got at cross-purposes with the MR they might make his position difficult.

Wagons at Tytherington Quarry *c.*1910. 'ED' on the wagons' sides denotes Engineer's Department. The handbrake is one side only. *M.J. Tozer Collection*

A 2 ft gauge locomotive at Grovesend Quarry *c.*1935. *W. Hurcombe Collection*

Messrs Sturge advised Hardwicke to forgo all claim for damages in consideration of a reduction in his carriage rates of 1*d*. per ton, which on 30,000 would amount to £125 annually, this might be made up to the MR by increased traffic to the advantage of both parties. On receiving this advice, Hardwicke telegraphed to Green QC saying that he would forgo all claim in consideration of a reduction in carriage of 1*d*. per ton. The outcome of this is not known.

The first engine to shunt Church Quarry was *Iron Duke*, a conventional road traction engine converted to 4-2-0. This was replaced by *Daphne*, a Peckett 0-4-0ST of 1899, Works No. 737, purchased new and eventually sold to Pilkington Bros, St Helen's, Lancashire in 1923. *Daphne* was replaced by *Catherine*, a 0-4-0ST built by Hunslet in 1882, Works No. 282, and obtained in January 1919 from the Admiralty Shipyard, Portbury. Traffic in the West Quarry was worked by a steam crane. Internal 2 ft gauge rail traffic at both quarries ceased by 1948 as it had been replaced by road haulage.

Grovesend Quarry situated between Tytherington and Grovesend tunnels, was also owned by Hardwicke. The Private Siding Agreement was dated 17th May, 1888, the siding laid 26th June, 1888 and brought into use by 4th July, 1888. On 31st March, 1904 a Private Siding Agreement was made with Aird & Co. to lengthen the siding and convert it into a loop. This was done in connection with the quarry's first major contract - stone supplies for the construction of the Royal Edward Dock at Avonmouth 1902-8 carried out by John Aird. A small mobile stone crusher was used at the quarry from 1902 and steam drills introduced in 1904. Sixty to 65 railway wagons carrying about 8 tons each were sent to Avonmouth weekly. During World War I the quarry was taken over by the Road Board and stone dispatched by rail. In post-war years the Teign Valley Granite Co. took over the quarry, installed overhead loading machinery, laid additional sidings and made a Private Siding Agreement on 7th March, 1921. Apart from stone, Tarmac was forwarded and a considerable tonnage of coal arrived for quarry consumption. Until the 1950s, granite arrived from the parent company's quarry at Trusham, Devon. On one day each year, ganger George Clutterbuck, employed by the LMS, stopped and obtained the signature of every lorry driver entering Grovesend Quarry in order that the railway retained the right of ownership of the land on which the lorries stood. A Private Siding Agreement was made with Roads Reconstruction (1934) Ltd on 7th July, 1958 and the agreement terminated on 30th September, 1967, following which the line closed. By 1956 an electric weighing machine enabled trucks to be weighed when travelling up to a speed of 4 mph. The quarry used a tractor for internal shunting.

Locomotives used on the 2 ft Gauge Railway at Grovesend Quarry

Loco. No.	*Type*	*Maker*	*Works No.*	*Built*	*Source*	*Disposal*
-	4 wheel*	John Fowler	7958	1898	New	Sold out of service
41	0-4-2ST	Kerr, Stuart	3065	1918	(a)	To New Frome Quarry after 7.1933.
-	0-4-0T	Avonside	2073	1933	(b)	To Cranmore Depot 4.1949
3	0-4-0WT	Barclay	1855	1931	(b)	To Cranmore Depot 4.1949
D8	0-4-0DM	Deutz	9898	1931	New	To Vobster Quarries 4.1949

* Class A4 Compound geared locomotive.

(a) Ex-Cranmore Depot pre-December 1928.

(b) Ex-Messrs Pugsley, contractors, *circa* November 1941. This engine had previously belonged to Durham County Water Board.

Class '4F' 0-6-0 No. 44424, with a train consisting of loaded ballast wagons from Tytherington Quarry, stops at Latteridge crossing for fireman Gordon Shortman to open the gates, 22nd August, 1956. Driver Percy Mills looks out of cab. *Author*

Class '4F' 0-6-0 No. 44569 of 82E (Bristol, Barrow Road), at Latteridge with an up goods train on 25th October, 1963. Opening one set of gates allowed just sufficient clearance. *W.F. Grainger*

Class '4F' 0-6-0 No. 44569 emerges from Tytherington tunnel into Grovesend Quarry, April 1963.
W.F. Grainger

In April 1963 No. 44569 returning from Thornbury has left empty bogie bolster wagons and the brake van on the main line and is picking up loaded stone hopper wagons from the quarry siding. Tony Vaisey is the travelling shunter. *W.F. Grainger*

Type '4' 'Peak' class diesel locomotive No. 192 heads a train over the Iron Acton by-pass crossing on 14th September, 1973. The change of gradient is noticeable. *W.H. Harbor/Author's Collection*

Brush type '4' locomotive No. 1608 approaches the by-pass with empties for Tytherington Quarry, 14th September, 1973. *W.H. Harbor/Author's Collection*

Although the March 1937 Working Time Table Appendix said that not exceeding 15 wagons may be propelled from Thornbury to Grovesend Quarry, with a brake van at the leading end, this method of working was rare. The usual way of working the siding was that *en route* between Thornbury and Yate, wagons and brake van were left on the main line while the engine picked up the loaded stone wagons and proceeded through Tytherington tunnel. As the engine and loaded wagons could not readily reverse up the 1 in 64 to collect the brake van and wagons left on the main line, some drivers arranged with the guard that the engine would work the six or seven loaded ballast wagons through to Tytherington where it would wait. The guard would then let the brake van and the remainder of the train run down the gradient and join the ballast wagons at Tytherington station. On one occasion the guard failed to stop the train in time, crashed into the ballast wagons, his own van falling apart and his injuries causing him to go to hospital.

The quarry gave the drivers a 7*s*. 6*d*. tip weekly to be shared equally by his fireman and the guard. Those working Christmas week were lucky as they received 10*s*. each.

Quarry Traffic Subsequent to Re-opening

Initially after re-opening in 1972, stone at Tytherington was loaded from ground stock pile by two Caterpillar CAT980 loading shovels each with a 4 cubic yard capacity bucket. On 20th July, 1973 new rail loading equipment, designed and installed by Crone & Taylor Ltd and the first of its kind in the United Kingdom, came into operation. The conception of this plant started when ARC decided to convert the major output of Tytherington back to rail and discussions led to the notion of a rapid stone loading terminal whereby a train could be accepted and released rapidly. The main criteria included:

a. Adequate railside storage to ensure immediate readiness pending train arrivals.
b. Provision for a possible variety of wagon load, of 16, 21, 26 and 37½ tons - no mean feat for a required loading rate of 1,500 tons per hour and an accuracy of + or - ½%.
c. The new system had to be provided within a strict budget as the cost of stone was very low and transportation costs exceed the product cost almost two-fold.
d. The plant had to be carefully sited to avoid a situation where a locomotive had more than half a loaded train on a gradient of 1 in 60 where it might be overwhelmed by the weight.

The new crushing and screening plants consisted of six 200 tonne capacity rail bins supplying any required grade of aggregate to railway wagons via conveyor belts and a 65 ft long travelling shuttle conveyor with an hydraulic luffing head distributing stone along a wagon's length.The luffing head was arranged so that in the lowered position it minimises dust nuisance and in the raised position it cleared the BR loading gauge. It was the finest equipment in the country for offering low cost of production combined with high efficiency.

An important feature of the plant was its electrical weighing system coupled to both the storage bins and the ground stock reclaim system, which ensured that all materials were weighed prior to loading, thus enabling wagons to be filled to capacity without any risk of overloading. Before loading the operator

Tytherington Quarry 24th August, 2000: loading siding, *right*; run-round loop, *left*; view west 24th August, 2000. *Author*

The end of the line, 10th April, 1991. The line was raised here from its original level to make the gradient less severe. The line to Thornbury led through the central arch into Grovesend tunnel. *Author*

makes a careful check that all the bottom discharge doors are firmly closed. Loading a 1,200 tonne train by conveyor belt takes about two hours and approximately the same time if loaded from ground with mechanical shovels.

A signal is placed towards the north end of the loading loop. Normally extinguished, a steady white light indicates to the locomotive driver that he should move forward slowly so that the next wagon can come below the conveyor belt feeding gantry. When the light is switched out this indicates 'Stop' because the next wagon is in the correct position. A flashing light means 'Set back slowly'. When only about three wagons remain to be loaded, at least six wagon hand brakes are applied, the engine uncoupled, run round and attached to the Yate end of the train. The hand brakes are then released, a white light comes on in the signal at the Yate end of the loop and the locomotive pushes a wagon below the loading gantry.

In October 1973 the quarry dispatched seven trains each 24 hours, the average capacity of a train being 650 tonnes. The destinations were:

3 trains daily to Wolverton - this depot had the largest throughput of aggregates of any railhead in the country. Milton Keynes' roads are based on Tytherington stone.

1 train daily to Hendon for the M1 extension.

2 trains daily to Redditch - for general trade because of the shortage of good quality stone south of Birmingham.

1 train daily to Kidlington - at first for building the M40, then for general trade.

Initially trains from Yate ran into the head shunt and returned back on to the loading line when the previous train had left.

When a loaded train arrives at Yate, if proceeding northwards the engine would use the run-round loop before reaching the main line, then propel the train to the up line and depart to Gloucester. Southbound trains run over the bi-directional up line to Westerleigh West Junction, there regain the down line, and if proceeding towards Swindon, run round at Stoke Gifford.

Initially 35 wagons, 21 tonne capacity and 29 tonnes gross, and formerly used for house coal concentration, were filled by shovel tractors which took about 1½ hours to load a train. A brake van was provided at each end to avoid having to run the van around its train for a return trip.

ARC discovered that by using its own wagons rather than those made available by BR, it could exercise greater control over aggregate distribution as well as operating a more economic service; so 4-wheeled wagons were built for ARC by Charles Roberts & Co. to a design by Procor Ltd. They were fitted with pedestal suspension and Girling-Westinghouse air-operated disc brakes. The power-operated doors made by Miner Enterprises Inc., Chicago, took advantage of the rapid bottom-discharge facilities available at ARC's depots. Each wagon carried a maximum payload of 37 tonnes - a total of 888 tonnes for a 24-wagon train. During the first year following the branch re-opening, 1,000 trains carrying in excess of 600,000 tonnes of stone were forwarded, equivalent to 45,000 lorries each with a load of 15 tonnes.

In 1984 two stone trains were run daily to the ARC terminal at Wolverton, Bucks and one daily to Allington, Kent; Appleford, Oxon; Theale, Berks and one of railway ballast to Woking. The gross weight of a train of 36 hopper wagons was about 2,000 tonnes and was hauled by either two class '37s', or one class '56'.

No. 59203 *Vale of Pickering* near the mouth of Tytherington tunnel while running round its train destined to Fareham, 24th August, 2000. *Author*

No. 59203 *Vale of Pickering* hauling trucks under the loading plant, 24th August, 2000. On the left are the six 'rail bins', of stone for loading. *Author*

The 1987 production at Tytherington was about 1.5 million tonnes, of which 1 million tonnes was dispatched by rail, weekly tonnages ranging from 20,000 to 23,000. Allington and Wolverton depots were supplied, each receiving two trains daily Mondays to Fridays.

Stone traffic ceased in January 1991 and the branch was mothballed in the first week of March, but re-opened for irregular traffic 12th March, 1991. As a result of less stone being required for the construction industry during the recession, it was mothballed again from mid-February 1992 and over the next few years was opened and closed periodically. Following two years of disuse, when opened on 9th January, 1995 with No. 58050 in 'Mainline' livery heading a train of Gunnells (four-wheeled 51 tonne gross wagons), a rail awareness programme had to be carried out as the locals had treated the line as a playground. That year Mainline Freight received a contract to transport 300,000 tonnes of stone obviating the need for 25,000 lorry journeys. Following this burst of traffic there was a lull, but but on 21st October, 1996 traffic was resumed when No. 59101 arrived with stone from Whatley for distribution by road.

The line continued to experience intermittent use. At the beginning of March 1999, five trains of stone scalp were run from Whatley to Tytherington in order to reduce the stockpile at Whatley. Locomotives experienced difficulties in retaining adhesion on the bank between Tytherington village and the tunnel. On one occasion the driver and trainman had to get down and sprinkle sand on the rails by hand in order to achieve adhesion. The scalpings were unloaded by Hanson's own 360 degrees track machine with clam shell bucket which cleared one wagon at a time. ARC changed its name to Hanson on 19th January, 1999.

No. 59203 *Vale of Pickering* immediately prior to running round its train to Fareham, 24th August, 2000. *Author*

From September 1999 the branch was re-opened yet again with approximately twice-weekly trains. In August 2000 a daily train was run to the Battersea terminal carrying stone aggregate, and another to Fareham for road building. Trains normally consisted of 18 wagons carrying a total of 1,200 tonnes.

Wagon stock used by Hanson in 2000

JHA 102 tonne gross wagons, bottom discharge
JUA PTA 102 tonne gross wagons, solid bottoms
JNA (Naccom boxes) 102 tonnes gross, solid bottoms
KPA 90 tonne gross, bottom discharge (owned by Tiphook)

At the time of writing (November 2001) the regular outgoing train to Battersea normally consists of MBA 102 tonne gross EWS box wagons hauled by an EWS class '66' locomotive. Less frequent traffic, such as that to Allington, is carried in JHA 51 tonne gross EWS four-wheeled hoppers. The occasional 'coals to Newcastle' train of stone from Whatley Quarry to Tytherington Quarry uses a Mendip Rail locomotive.

Maximum speed on the branch is limited to 20 mph.

No. 59203 *Vale of Pickering*, driver Andrew Gentle and trainman Robin Hull. Their bags have been unloaded to take to the other cab when the train is run round, 24th August, 2000. *Author*

Chapter Six

Locomotives and Working

Steam Era

No record exists of the type of locomotive which worked the branch in the early days, but it is likely that an 0-6-0 would have been required to handle the ascents and descents of goods trains over the steep gradients. Certainly some passenger trains were worked by Johnson class '1P' 0-4-4'Ts, No. 1825 being recorded in 1892 and No. 1388 *circa* 1907. In the 1920s a 0-4-4T was stabled at Thornbury. During April 1932 class '3F' 0-6-0T No. 16761 and No. 16762 replaced class '1P' 0-4-4Ts on Bristol to Thornbury passenger trains.

From 1934 class '3F' 0-6-0s handled much of the traffic. For instance in 1938 the 6.20 pm Bristol (Temple Meads) to Thornbury was often headed by an engine of this class. On arrival at Thornbury, coal in the tender was shovelled forward, the engine moved to the water crane for the tank to be filled and the fire cleaned before the engine was left in the shed overnight. Class '3F' Nos. 3419 and 3727 were regular Thornbury branch engines in 1941, only one being stationed there at a time. Class '4F' 0-6-0 No. 4134 also put in an appearance.

During the post-World War II years, the locomotive working the branch freight tended to be a class '4F' 0-6-0, but class '3Fs' appeared, including No. 43194 on 19th November, 1957, ex-Somerset & Dorset Joint Railway No. 62 of 71H, Templecombe, a Southern Region-allocated engine. Ivatt class '4MT' 2-6-0s occasionally appeared, including Nos. 43012 and 43013 shedded at Barrow Road. Class '2MT' No. 41240 headed the weed-killing train on 10th April, 1962. On 18th January, 1965 class '5' 4-6-0 No. 45280 worked the branch goods and so did class '8F' 2-8-0 No. 48458, on 1st December, 1964, class '4F' 0-6-0 No. 44466 having failed on the road and the second choice, a 'Black Five' 4-6-0 failed on shed! No. 48458 was a Mold Junction engine, recently ex-works with a white star painted on the cab side denoting that its wheels were balanced for working fitted freights. A class '2P' 4-4-0 appeared on a weed-killing train.

In the BR era the following steam engines have been recorded as working over the branch:

Class '2MT' 2-6-2T: No. 41240
Class '3F' 0-6-0: Nos. 43194, 43593, 43825
Class '4F' 0-6-0: Nos. 43837, 43887, 43924, 43932, 43951, 43963, 43979, 44040, 44047, 44112, 44131, 44135, 44137, 44160, 44165, 44179, 44180, 44187, 44211, 44235, 44255, 44256, 44264, 44269, 44355, 44371, 44411, 44414, 44419, 44424, 44466, 44472, 44534, 44535, 44569, 44583
Class '4MT' 2-6-0: Nos. 43012, 43013, 43046
Class '5' 4-6-0: No. 45280
Class '8' 2-8-0: No. 48458
BR Standard class '3' 2-6-2T: No. 82001
BR Standard class '4' 4-6-0: No. 75001
BR Standard class '5' 4-6-0: No. 73015
BR (WR) '16XX' class 0-6-0PT: No. 1625
Ex-GWR '2251' class 0-6-0: No. 2229
Ex-GWR '5101' class 2-6-2T: No. 4103
Ex-GWR '57XX' class 0-6-0PT: Nos. 3659, 3696, 3752, 9680

Class '1P' 0-4-4T No. 1339 at Bristol (Temple Meads) following arrival with a through train from Thornbury, 4th March, 1928. *Colin Roberts Collection*

Class '3F' 0-6-0T No. 16761 at Bristol, Barrow Road Shed on 26th June, 1932. At this period it worked Bristol to Thornbury passenger trains. *Colin Roberts Collection*

Although engine working over the branch tended to be allocated to Bristol, Barrow Road, it was not exceptional for one to be seen from such sheds as Coalville, Derby, Saltley or Toton. One branch driver preferred the Midland Railway Fowler class '4Fs' to those of the LMS, claiming that they steamed better: 'You could thrash them and have both injectors on and they would still blow off'.

During World War II, in November 1941 ex-London & South Western Railway Drummond 'K10' class mixed traffic 4-4-0s Nos. 135, 388 389 were shedded at Barrow Road and tended to work the Thornbury goods. Initially classified '2P', No. 135 left Bristol in August 1944 for Nottingham and eventually arrived back on the SR at the end of 1944 classified '2F'. Nos. 388 and 389 remained at Bristol until March 1945.

Locomotive Load Limit 1st July, 1886

Thornbury to Tytherington:	
Double frame engines:	16 minerals; 20 goods; 30 empties
Single frame engines:	19 minerals; 24 goods; 36 empties
Tytherington to Yate Junction:	
Double frame engines:	30 minerals; 37 goods; 50 empties
Single frame engines:	36 minerals; 44 goods; 50 empties
Yate to Thornbury:	
Double frame engines:	16 minerals; 20 goods; 30 empties
Single frame engines:	19 minerals; 24 goods; 36 empties

When descending the steep banks between Thornbury and Iron Acton in either direction, one wagon break [*sic*] must be pinned down for every three wagons above twelve.

In 1928 a typical day started with the class '3F' 0-6-0 shedded at Thornbury leaving at 8.00 am with the through passenger train to Bristol (Temple Meads). The return working arrived at Thornbury 10.17 am. A passenger train just to Yate left at 10.40 am. As there was no passenger train around midday, this allowed the '3F' to work a freight from Yate to Thornbury and back. The engine then left Yate at 3.22 pm with a passenger train to Thornbury, returning with the 4.50 pm through to Bristol (Temple Meads), leaving there at 6.20 pm and arriving Thornbury 7.15 pm. On market day at Thornbury, the second Wednesday of the month, the down freight included empty passenger coaches which worked back as a 2.30 pm mixed train Thornbury to Yate in the path of the usual freight train.

The first ex-GWR engine to work over the branch seems to have been '2251' class 0-6-0 No. 2229 which hauled breakdown coach D198623 (ex-Lancashire & Yorkshire Railway) to Tytherington on 13th July, 1961. '57XX' class 0-6-0PT No. 3752 worked the first trip on 3rd April, 1962, but failed at Tytherington, No. 44135 being sent to haul it back to Barrow Road. On 14th March, 1963 ex-GWR '5101' class 2-6-2T No. 4103 was tried over the line with a special train of 26 16-ton loaded coal wagons. It experienced difficulty in climbing the gradient through Tytherington and was not used subsequently. On 6th February, 1964

Class '4F' 0-6-0 No. 44355 at Thornbury, 17th August 1956. *Author*

Driver Frank Jones can be seen on the footplate of '4F' class 0-6-0 No. 44536 as it stands on the turntable at Thornbury, 18th March, 1955. *Russell Leitch*

In September 1963 class '4F' 0-6-0 No. 44296 is turned by driver Roger Kilminster at Thornbury. Notice the storm sheet between the cab roof and tender. *W.F. Grainger*

Class '3P' 2-6-2T No. 40164, of 22A (Bristol, Barrow Road), recently returned from Horwich Works is seen at Yate on 18th April, 1952, it is running round coaches which had formed the 8.20 am Bristol (Temple Meads) to Yate. *Colin Roberts*

Thornbury shed. *D.K. Jones/Roger Griffiths Collection*

The interior of the former engine shed at Thornbury, 1962. *W.F. Grainger*

ex-GWR '57XX' class 0-6-0PT No. 3659 was used on the branch train and also appeared with a weed-killing train on 21st February, 1964. No. 9680 of the same class was in charge of the freight on 14th August, 1965, as well as a '94XX' class 0-6-0PT on 19th June, 1965.

In 1962 the volume of traffic exceeded what a single class '4F' could handle and as a number of ex-London & North Western Railway class '7F' 0-8-0s were stored out of use in the Wigan area, it was suggested through the Yate station master that some of these could be obtained to ease the situation. The Divisional Office declined to follow up this situation because the locomotives belonged to another Region!

On 26th February, 1965 class '4F' 0-6-0 No. 44269 worked the last regular steam-hauled trip to Thornbury.

Thornbury Shed

In Midland Railway days, Thornbury Shed, a sub-shed of Bristol had the code 8b. A single road 'temporary' timber building erected as cheaply as possible, it was built *circa* 1872. A tank and water supply was provided the same year at a cost of £400. Fed from a spring by Grovesend Quarry, the water ran through the tunnel. An overflow was situated at the Thornbury end of the tunnel and watercress flourished here and was enjoyed by railwaymen, short goods trains sometimes stopping so that it could be picked. This was not done with a longer train because of the problem of re-starting on the gradient. Grovesend water, in addition to supplying locomotives, also provided for The Bathings - a cold water bathing pool owned by a smallholder to supplement his income. The supply also provided water to Grace's saw mill at Thornbury.

Thornbury Shed was the only locomotive water supply on the branch. The fireman placed the bag in the tender and pulled the handle down. Although a tender of water lasted a long time, he topped it up during the day and arranged, if being relieved, to have a full tank ready for the new crew. On at least one occasion, in the 1930s, the Barrow Road outdoor machinery foreman Albert Nevitt, took several cleaners to Thornbury to clean out the water tank. After draining the water, moss and weeds were scraped off the tank sides and bottom.

The shed closed with the withdrawal of the passenger train service on 19th June, 1944, freight locomotives working out from Barrow Road. From 1st October, 1946 the coal merchant E.G. Watts paid a rental for garaging his lorry in the former engine shed. The locomotive siding and rails to the shed were lifted in December 1948. In 1956 rails were still laid inside the shed, but were unconnected with the rest of the layout.

There was no direct access to the shed from the run-round loop, an engine having first to run to the turntable road and then reverse across the goods yard shunting neck at an angle. Adjacent to the shed road was a siding for the locomotive coal and ash wagons. The locomotive coal wagons' siding was at a slightly higher level than the shed road to make the transfer of coal easier. Two wagons of Derby or Blidworth coal were used weekly. During World War II briquettes made from Welsh coal and bitumen were used. An engine was coaled using a shovel to transfer the coal from a wagon direct into the tender. If an opportunity arose to visit Barrow Road Shed, labour was saved by filling the tender with coal from the hopper of the coal plant.

Thornbury had two drivers and two firemen, the latter being passed firemen and required to know the road between Thornbury and Bristol St Philip's and Temple Meads, so that in the event of a driver being ill, he could take over this driving turn and have a fireman sent from Bristol. One Bristol fireman sent on relief took a bell tent, his wife and two children to Thornbury on a privilege ticket and they camped there for the week, but many firemen would often sleep in the porters' room at Thornbury station. Apart from saving money, this was more convenient for getting up to book on at 4.30 am to raise steam. The fire had been cleaned right out because overnight the engine was left unattended. An engine never became really cold. The next morning the fireman put a few fire-lighters in the box and soon raised steam before his driver booked on. During the 1940s, on one occasion when a Bristol fireman was unavailable, Sam Collins, the Thornbury porter, was allowed to travel on the footplate with the driver as far as Yate where a fireman from Bristol took over. Sam was familiar with steam from having driven Sentinel and Foden steam wagons before joining the railway.

In passenger train days the branch engine was changed weekly. The locomotive working the 10.15 am Thornbury to Yate shunted the coaches to the looped siding on the inside curve of the branch, travelled light to Barrow Road and a fresh engine was brought back together with a supply of paraffin, lubricating oil and fire lighters. There was no cleaner at Thornbury, so an engine only got cleaned when it returned to Barrow Road.

Railwaymen enjoyed a few unofficial perks. Lineside gangers sometimes gave orders to footplate crews to buy cigarettes at Yate, or pick up a parcel, and it was not unknown for a fireman to cut bean sticks while the driver and guard were shunting. One Thornbury driver in charge of a passenger train carried a gun on his footplate and on one occasion, shortly after leaving Thornbury, shot a rabbit and retrieved it without stopping his train.

Locomotives Loading for the Thornbury Branch, 1st October, 1945

	Passenger						*Freight*			
Class of engine	1	2	3	4	5	5X	2	3	4	5
Loads in tons	115	155	190	210	240	275	165	200	230	265

Note: Passenger trains were still catered for in the table although the passenger service was withdrawn on 19th June, 1944.

Among the unusual engines which passed through Yate on the main line were:

No. 92045 BR Standard '9F' class 2-10-0 (Toton), the first appearance of this class, November 1955.

No. 64789 ex-LNER 'J39' class 0-6-0 (Spital Bridge, Peterborough), 10th October, 1959.

No. 60954 ex-LNER 'V2' class 2-6-2 (York) believed to have worked a freight Washwood Heath to Westerleigh Sidings 16th November, 1959 and certainly returned light the next day.

No. 42182 '4MT' class 2-6-4T (Leicester) worked a freight from Gloucester to Stoke Gifford 21st November, 1959.

No. 60839 ex-LNER 'V2' class 2-6-2 (York) worked freight to Westerleigh, 11th December, 1959.

(About this period, ex-LNER 'B1' 4-6-0s appeared approximately weekly on express passenger, fitted freight and local passenger trains.)

No. 46164 *The Artists' Rifleman* 'Royal Scot' class 4-6-0 (Millhouses, Sheffield) worked the down 'Devonian' instead of the usual Holbeck 'Jubilee', 23rd July, 1960.

No. 63675 ex-LNER '04/8' 2-8-0 (Colwick) worked a train of concrete sleepers Colwick to Highbridge as far as Stoke Gifford 18th November, 1960.

No. 6229 *Duchess of Hamilton* 'Coronation' class 4-6-2 *en route* behind 'Grange' class 4-6-0 No. 6825 *Llanvair Grange* from Crewe to Minehead via Stratford-upon-Avon and Mangotsfield. Over the Midland line the train was classed as an 'out of gauge load', 20th April, 1964. The engine had been bought by Butlin's of Minehead as an exhibit.

In the mid-1960s processions of dead engines *en route* to South Wales for scrapping were a regular occurrence. For safety reasons none were allowed through the Severn tunnel and so had to be routed via Gloucester. On 16th June, 1964 for instance, ex-SR 'U' class 2-6-0 No. 31618 was noted at Yate towing a string of Southern engines and the following day an SR 'Q1' class 0-6-0 towed three of its classmates. On another day, 27th January, 1965, 'Z' class 0-8-0T No. 30952 was detached at Yate from a train of dead engines because an axlebox had run hot and required attention from the carriage and wagon department before proceeding to John Cashmore Ltd, Newport.

The author 'oiling' No. 44355 at Thornbury, 17th August, 1956. *Author*

The Diesel Era

The first diesel engine on the branch was probably 0-6-0 shunter No. D4022 which worked the train on 4th April, 1962 with a load equal to 25 wagons of mineral. The same engine hauled the Engineer's inspection coach to Thornbury on 22nd November, 1962, while on 22nd May, 1963 No. D3187 was in charge of the tunnel inspection train to Tytherington. Type '1' diesel-hydraulic 0-6-0 No. 9502 was the branch engine on 3rd August, 1965. The first regular diesels on the branch were 'Hymeks'. These started on Monday 1st March, 1965, No. D7049 working on that date, No. D7050 appearing the following day. The Fison's weed-killing train to Thornbury on 30th April, 1965 was headed by No. D7056, though several subsequent Saturday turns were steam-hauled: 0-6-0PT No. 8403 on 19th June, 1965; Standard class '3' 2-6-2T No. 82001 on 3rd July, 1965 and 0-6-0PT No. 9680 on 14th August, 1965.

Dmu driving second No. 56287 and motor brake second No. 55034 were used in July and August 1972 to enable drivers to learn the road. The engine of the first train after re-opening was Brush type '4' No. 1857. Since then quite a variety of engines have appeared. At one time the heaviest trains were hauled by two class '37s', or one class '56', while lighter trains were headed by a class '45', class '46', class '47' or two class '25s', two class '31s' or two class '33s'. Class '59s' have been used. No. 60041 was tested on 23rd December, 1991 and class '60s' passed to work over the branch. The train to Woking was regularly hauled by a single class '33'. Class '58' No. 58136 was noted heading a train on 24th and 25th July, 1995. The class '66' first ran on the branch in September 1999.

The loading control cabin at Tytherington Quarry: the overall total weight counter in the far corner; individual wagon load recorder in the foreground, 24th August, 2000. *Author*

Chapter Seven

Signalling, Permanent Way and Mishaps

Signalling

The original Yate Junction signal box closed on 9th March, 1886, and was replaced by two new boxes:Yate Main Line Junction and Yate Single Line Junction. The former, in addition to the main line, controlled the entrance and exit from the Thornbury branch. During 1916-17, north of Yate station No. 3 (Western) Aircraft Repair Depot was established. The additional traffic required Yate Main Line Junction signal box to be extended in February 1919 by 12 levers, making a total of 40, of which three were spare; while in addition a ground stage was installed with six levers electrically interlocked and released from the signal box. Yate Main Line box was reduced to a ground frame on 20th October, 1969 by which time the Thornbury branch had been lifted. The ground frame closed on 10th May, 1971 when the sidings, formerly part of the Thornbury branch, were taken out of use. Yate Single Line Junction signal box opened on 9th March, 1886 and was situated at the end of the double track 264 yards from the main line. It closed on 8th October, 1905 when the loop was extended to about 440 yards and a replacement box opened. It was probably around this date that 'Junction' was dropped from the title of Yate Main Line signal box. As an economy measure, from 14th November, 1926 the layout was, modified so that the branch was single line to its junction with the main line, the former ¼-mile of the down branch line becoming a siding. Branch trains ran in both directions over the former up line. As a train entered or left the Yate track-circuited section, it rang a bell in the Main Line signal box. From 14th November, 1926 the site of the other box became Yate Single Line Junction ground frame until taken out of use on 18th December, 1966. On that date this length of track was taken out of use and the whole branch worked as a siding, trains running over a line running parallel with what had been until 1926 the up and down branch lines. The staff had a key at one end to unlock the ground frame.

The branch was initially worked by train staff between Yate and Iron Acton and 'One engine in steam' Iron Acton to Thornbury until 1876-77 when the whole branch was worked by train staff. The Working Time Table Appendix for March 1937 described the staff as 'round and black'. The person appointed to receive it was the signalman at Yate Main Line and the station master at Thornbury. The branch was operated on the system of one engine in steam, or two coupled together. On at least two occasions in steam days the staff was lost. It was general practice for the guard to have the staff on the outward journey in order to work the frame at Grovesend Quarry and then he often left it on the verandah of his van. On returning from Thornbury, and about to re-open the ground frame at Grovesend Quarry, he found it missing. Eventually after a thorough search it was discovered protruding from water in a nearby lineside trough where it had fallen after being vibrated off. A similar thing

Left: A driver hands the single line staff to the Thornbury station master *c.*1920. *Author's Collection*

Above: The Thornbury branch staff and key.

Below: The Yate to Tytherington tablet, 24th August, 2000. *Author*

Below: At Thornbury driver Roger Kilminster holds the single line staff and is accompanied by fireman Royston Tucker, September 1963. *W.F. Grainger*

happened on another occasion, the staff was never found and a replacement had to be made.

Sometimes a driver forgot the staff and left it in the ground frame at Grovesend Quarry. In such a situation, the wagons were uncoupled and left at Yate while he returned light engine to fetch it. In the days of one freight train a day only, he had to beware of cows and horses, as some farmers loosed animals on to the embankments to graze after the daily train had passed.

Following closure of the branch on 30th September, 1967 the track was lifted beyond the ¾ mile post. With the branch's restoration, on the opposite side of the line to where Yate Main Line signal box had been, Yate Middle ground frame was opened on 3rd July, 1972 to give access to the relaid branch which led off the main up line, trains from the branch running south also using it as it was signalled for two-way working. This ground frame was released from the Bristol panel box. Although the actual junction at Yate is single, the branch soon bifurcates into double to allow a Tytherington-bound train to pass an outward-bound one waiting to proceed to the main line.

Iron Acton station signal box opened by 16th August, 1877, was re-framed on 16th June, 1907 and on 19th June, 1928 reduced to a ground frame unlocked by the single line staff. When a passenger train left any branch station, a red button beside the telegraph was pressed to give the next station warning of its approach.

Iron Acton and Latteridge level crossings were both protected by distant signals and latterly these were the only signals on the branch. Following the withdrawal of passenger traffic, Tytherington distant signals were removed on 21st November, 1944. To save expense, after the withdrawal of the passenger service, train crews operated the gates instead of the occupants of the crossing cottages. As it had no water supply, the lodge at Latteridge crossing received a churn of water carried on the first passenger train of the day.

The Admiralty Stone Siding south of Tytherington was accessed at the south end by No. 1 ground frame and No. 2 ground frame at the north end. At Tytherington station another ground frame offered admission to the quarry sidings, but was taken out of use in October 1963. Grovesend Quarry loop had a ground frame at each end. Thornbury signal box opened by 16th August, 1877 and closed on 26th October, 1886. Its replacement was a point box (a covered ground frame), situated at the station throat.

A special blasting signal was situated about 350 yards on the Iron Acton side of Tytherington. If blasting at the West Quarry was imminent and likely to put rock on the line, this signal, worked by a wheel and chain, was operated to give warning. On one occasion class '3F' 0-6-0 No. 3727, a Thornbury engine, once had the overflow of the injector on the fireman's side broken when struck by a rock thrown by blasting.

Following the line's restoration in 1972, on the arrival of a train at Yate, the engine stops at a light operated from the Bristol panel box. At Middle ground frame the trainman makes contact with the Bristol panel and is given a release to take the single line staff out and then uses it to unlock the ground frame. The driver then moves forward on to the branch and stops by the marker board for the number of wagons indicated. The trainman replaces the ground frame levers and gives the driver the staff.

Class '4F' 0-6-0 No. 44296 at Yate Single Line ground frame, September 1963. *W.F. Grainger*

Latteridge crossing up fixed distant signal seen from the cab of class '4F' 0-6-0 No. 44569, 1963. *W.F. Grainger*

Iron Acton level crossing is protected by flashing lights, and the Iron Acton by-pass and Latteridge crossings, by lifting barriers. For the two latter crossings a train halts at a stop board and the trainman unlocks a cupboard and pushes the 'Lower' button. A yellow light flashes on the crossing and the barrier drops and a white light flashes on the control post where the trainman is operating. The train proceeds over the crossing and approximately a train-length away from the crossing a 'BU' (barriers up) illuminated sign indicates that the barriers have been automatically raised and are free to road traffic. Should the sign not light up, the trainman has to return and press the 'Raise' button and if the barriers still fail to function, he has to pump them up manually. Today an engine on the branch carries two drivers, one of whom carries out the trainmen's duties.

The Thornbury branch was part of a local circuit of the LMS internal phone, system and included Yate South Junction and Yate Main Line signal boxes, Yate station booking office and Thornbury. Thornbury lost its railway maintained phone line from Yate *circa* 1950, it being cheaper to use the GPO system.

Permanent Way

In steam days rails were in 30, 45 and 60 ft lengths, the sleepers laid on ash ballast. Gangers would replace a bad sleeper while traffic was still running. In the autumn of 1961 several stretches were replaced with good second-hand rail in readiness for the heavier traffic expected for the construction of the Severn Bridge and Oldbury nuclear power station. Much of the track was previously of 30 ft length rails and some of the chairs at Thornbury were lettered LNWR. The two tunnels were examined annually and loose rock in the unlined portion removed by pick. In LMS days the tunnel van was based at Gloucester, but in the BR era it came from Ashton Gate, Bristol. In the event of a cutting being blocked by snow - that near the north end of Grovesend tunnel was particularly prone - either a plough was used, or the snow simply dug out manually.

It is recorded that in September 1945 the railway banks were gassed to destroy rabbits which were undermining the railway formation and the late Trevor Keedwell recalled that the embankment near Iron Acton was so undermined with rabbits' workings that the safety of trains was becoming endangered.

In 1946 the permanent way ganger walked the line once daily. Five men were in the gang based at Thornbury. They worked from about 7.15 am till 4.30 pm. For carrying materials they used a rail-mounted manually-pushed trolley and to avoid being struck by a train, a man walked ahead of it and on a train's approach, paced three detonators on the track to give warning in case the trolley could not be lifted off in time. When going down a gradient the men unofficially boarded the trolley and rode. Today the Charfield gang maintain the branch as well as the main line, travelling by road in a mess van.

The branch is maintained for 20 mph running. When the track was relaid in 1972 some flat-bottomed and some bullhead rail was used. The villagers at Tytherington complained of the noise when trains passed over rail joints at night, so those in the vicinity were welded. Today, a weed-killing train makes

View from the west end of the loop towards Tytherington Quarry. On the right can be seen a point lever and grease pot, 24th August, 2000. *Author*

Tytherington Quarry: view towards the end of the run-round loop, 24th August, 2000. The lamp to indicate movements is on the pole in the centre of the picture. *Author*

View of the cutting leading to Tytherington tunnel. The growth on either side causes leaf fall problems in autumn. When the photograph was taken on 10th April, 1991 the branch was temporarily closed. *Author*

Whistle notice and 15 mph restriction sign approaching Iron Acton crossing. In the foreground is the site of Iron Acton station, 10th April, 1991. *Author*

View south from the A38 of the shunting spur at Tytherington Quarry with the stop blocks in the foreground, 10th April, 1991. *Author*

Tytherington: expansion joint of welded rail, 10th April, 1991. *Author*

an annual visit and a machine is used to cut back foliage. The branch was originally protected mainly by a hawthorn hedge rather than a fence.

During World War II, south of Grovesend tunnel a bomb fell during Saturday night/Sunday morning destroying a length of track. By Monday morning the engineers had replaced it, though a speed restriction was imposed for a week to allow the ballast to settle.

The loop at Yate had to be carefully designed to fit into the 1,100 ft length between the trap points protecting the main line and bridge No. 2 to avoid the bridge having to be reconstructed for double track at an additional cost of £5,000.

When the track was relaid in 1972 materials came from the Mangotsfield to Bath branch and the former main line Mangotsfield to Fishponds. The permanent way had been lifted by a tracked crane (RB56) and taken to Westerleigh Yard on open flats by 0-6-0 diesel-electric shunter No. 3517. There it was stacked up to 14 lengths in height. Unfortunately the best flat-bottomed rail was required for continuous-welding main line use. Track laying on the Tytherington branch was by a crane drawing a panel from the end of the train and the latter passing over it as soon as the fishplates were bolted. The six miles of track were laid in about a week and then Tytherington Quarry was able to supply the ballast. Despite the rush, the contractor was absolutely first class and met all his dates on the reinstatement, coping well with minor irritants - such as engines booked for trains being sent elsewhere and wagons delayed in transit.

1. ALL accidents to loaded passenger trains.

2. Accidents to other trains, derailments, failures of engines, rolling stock, permanent way or works, signalling or block telegraph apparatus, and fires, which are either serious or delay important main line express passenger trains for more than 10 minutes or block main lines for more than 30 minutes.

3. Fatal or serious injuries to the public or staff.

4. Serious exceptional occurrences, such as trains narrowly escaping collision with other trains, vehicles or other obstructions, and vehicles running away.

The following information must be given:—

(a) Train or trains concerned, nature of accident, and TIME AND PLACE it occurred.

(b) Cause of accident.

(c) Personal injuries, if any.

(d) The lines that are blocked, how long the block is likely to continue, and, where only one line is blocked, whether single line is being worked.

The fact of the accident or obstruction must be IMMEDIATELY telegraphed, and, if necessary, a second message, giving details must follow. A further message must be sent when the lines have been cleared.

If the telegram is in connection with a fire a copy must be sent to the Divisional Fire Superintendent at ......Crewe......

A copy of the wire must also be sent to the Divisional Chemist at......Crewe......when:—

1. Dangerous goods are involved in a fire.

2. There are suspicious circumstances which point to the fire being due to other than external causes, e.g. spontaneous combustion, etc.

3. Where food stuffs or perishables are involved and chemical extinguishers have been employed.

NOTE.—Fires caused by the action of water on lime must not be reported to the Chemist.

In case of fire on or threatening the Railway Company's property an alarm must be given at once to the Company's local fire brigade by fire bell, whistle or other means.

The staff including signalmen, must make themselves fully acquainted with the diagram prepared by the Station Master, Goods Agent, or other supervisor indicating the positions of all hydrants, stop valves, drain cocks, by-pass valves, hose boxes, fire buckets and fire extinguishers and, when the fire is of such proportions that it cannot be readily extinguished by the Company's local fire brigade or other means are not available for successfully dealing with the outbreak, no delay must occur in ordering the Fire Brigade of the Local Authority at ......Local Fire Brigade Thornbury......

by ......Telephone. Post Office & Police......

and the Company's Fire Train at......Derby......

by......Telegram......to the District Control Office at......Gloucester......and if the District Control Office is closed, by......Telegram......

to the Divisional Control at......Derby......

....

The Company's Fire Train at......Derby......

consists of a motor-pump with a tank having a capacity for............

gallons of water and although a fire may be got under control quickly a considerable amount of salvage work may be necessary and this point must be borne in mind when determining whether the Fire Train is required or not for the latter purpose.

The District Passenger Manager or the District Goods and Passenger Manager at ......Bristol......

must be immediately advised by......Telegram......of—

(1) Any mishap to a passenger train where a passenger is seriously injured or a trainman fatally injured.

(2) Any mishap where passenger train traffic is damaged to any considerable extent.

(3) Any serious accident to a passenger or member of the Public on the Company's premises.

When goods or mineral traffic is involved in a train accident the Goods Agent at ......Thornbury......

must be advised at once by......Telephone......

If there is any evidence that an accident has been caused by a displaced or badly constructed load, the Goods Agent at......Thornbury......

must be advised at once by......Telephone......

and the District Goods Manager at......Bristol......

must be advised at once by wire or telephone.

Extract from form *Arrangements for dealing with Accident & Fire at Tytherington Station*, December 1934.

Mishaps

Fortunately the branch has been free from serious accident, most being of trains running through closed crossing gates. One such mishap occurred in early 1952 when the brake van and wagons were insufficiently secured when uncoupled at Iron Acton to allow the engine to shunt. They ran back through Latteridge crossing gates and came to a halt about half a mile beyond.

Point levers at Thornbury were of the Turk's head pattern, weighted near the top. To operate them correctly, they had to be pulled out before being thrown over. A WR guard once threw a lever over without pulling it out, with the result that after the locomotive had passed over, the points changed direction and the tender wheels were derailed. Fortunately there was a BR road vehicle at Yate which collected the train crew and single line staff, while Sam, the Thornbury porter, was sent up the line towards Grovesend tunnel to protect the train. At Yate the driver handed the single line staff to the driver of the breakdown train.

Around 1954, on returning from Thornbury, driver Cross reported an incident to Yate station master Ivan Barter. When returning through Tytherington tunnel his engine had struck an employee of the Tytherington Stone Co. taking a short cut through the tunnel on his way home. Fortunately the injury was not serious. It transpired that deafness prevented the trespasser from hearing the train's approach.

One day a train had passed Latteridge loop and was on the straight heading to Tytherington station with the class '4F' 0-6-0 moving briskly in readiness for the 1½ mile climb at 1 in 59-61, when a man was spotted displaying a red flag. The permanent way department working in Tytherington tunnel had a rail out and the Yate Main Line signalman had not been warned! As no further progress was possible, No. 44466 had to propel its train the five miles back to Yate.

When ex-GWR '57XX' class No. 3696 was returning from Thornbury on 4th March, 1965 following snow plough duty, as it entered Tytherington tunnel a bird sheltering there flew against cab on the fireman's side. He opened the window and picked the injured bird from the top of the pannier tank. Quite upset by the incident, he kept the bird inside his overall top for warmth hoping it would recover, but before long its injuries proved fatal.

Another fowl incident occurred around 1961. An engine was picking up loaded ballast hopper wagons at Tytherington, and, as usual, fowls from an adjacent small holding were running about. When the engine moved forward, a hen ran across the track in front of it. Unfortunately it did not quite clear the rail in time and one of its legs was severed. the bird, otherwise uninjured, hopped about on one leg. The, driver asked the Yate booking clerk to telephone the smallholder, who thanked him for ringing and said, 'The bird will be all right'.

Today drivers must remember not to set off too enthusiastically from Tytherington Quarry and then having to brake sharply on the down gradient of 1 in 58 through Tytherington tunnel. On the curve, the weight of the rear wagons, whose brakes come on a few seconds after those at the front, can derail those at the front. One such incident happened on 23rd March, 1995 when the tunnel was blocked and only freed when ARC equipment extricated the derailed vehicles.

Appendix One

Traffic at Tytherington (1941-1949)

Year	*Passengers*		*Parcels Traffic forwarded*	*Parcels Traffic received*	*Parcels Traffic revenue*	*Total coaching receipts*	*Total goods weight carted and not carted*	*Coal and coke*	*Other minerals*	*Total merchandise*	*Total goods receipts*	*Total coaching & goods receipts*
	No.	£	*No.*	*No.*	£	£	*tons*	*tons*	*tons*	*tons*	£	£
1941	5,915	196	137	222	27	223	93	2,865	53,899	56,857	18,625	18,848
1942	6,429	249	196	454	28	277	9	2,088	15,467	17,564	5,092	5,369
1943	5,982	263	198	395	32	295	74	2,796	14,020	16,890	6,038	6,333
1944	2,303*	80*	165	403	21	101	49	1,761	8,935	10,745	3,394	3,495
1945	-	-	137	353	22	22	15	2,207	12,818	15,040	4,761	4,783
1946	-	-	111	248	14	14	3	2,093	12,518	14,614	3,952	3,966
1947	-	-	64	14	10	10	13	2,522	5,441	7,976	2,021	2,031
1948	-	-	63	21	9	9	24	2,244	8,327	10,595	3,963	3,972
1949	-	-	26	11	4	4	18	1,348	7,987	9,355	3,439	3,443

Notes:

* Until 19th June, 1944.

Appendix Two

Traffic at Thornbury (1941-1954)

Year	*Passengers*		*Parcels Traffic forwarded*	*received*	*revenue*	*Horses*		*Total coaching receipts*	*Total goods weight carted and not carted*	*Coal and coke*	*Other minerals*	*Livestock*	*Total merchandise*	*Total goods receipts*	*Total coaching & goods receipts*
	No.	*£*	*No.*	*No.*	*£*	*No.*	*£*	*£*	*tons*	*tons*	*tons*	*No.*	*tons*	*£*	*£*
1941	6,330	211	1,526	5,470	307	11	5	523	695	8,731	109	191	9,774	763	1,286
1942	8,427	246	1,430	4,400	193	-	-	455	990	7,669	245	236	9,192	1,605	2,060
1943	4,055	271	1,936	5,045	276	-	-	547	1,667	7,807	9	543	10,078	2,280	2,827
1944	1,579*	87*	1,647	4,906	282	-	-	369	3,376	6,772	44	351	10,595	5,383	5,752
1945	-	-	1,367	4,394	255	-	-	255	2,812	6,534	190	159	9,750	3,394	3,649
1946	-	-	1,142	2,881	213	-	-	213	860	6,821	166	240	7,907	1,547	1,760
1947	-	-	564	239	99	1	4	103	519	8,185	117	124	8,952	840	943
1948	-	-	585	374	274	1	-	274	1,034	6,694	203	135	8,077	1,623	1,897
1949	-	-	486	293	95	2	2	97	1,006	6,811	2,917	75	10,809	3,058	3,155
1950	-	-	421	356	101	1	5	106	553	8,696	5,648	99	15,026	3,015	3,121
1951	-	-	334	398	66	1	3	69	321	9,104	427	15	9,887	1,512	1,581
1952	-	-	261	292	94	1	6†	122	1,345	9,025	4,980	75	70,009	2,293	2,415
1953	-	-	274	214	55	-	-	55	734	1,124	955	1,628	55,771	?	?
1954	-	-	291	284	40	-	-	40	851	105	520	625	42,283	1,022	1,062

Notes:

* Until 19th June, 1944
† Plus one carriage £22.

Appendix Three

Goods Traffic (1960s)

	RECEIVED General Merchandise		Minerals		Coal & Coke		Free-hauled*		FORWARDED General Merchandise		Minerals		Free-hauled*	
	Wagons	tons	wagons	tons	wagon	tons	wagons	tons	wagons	tons	wagons	tons	wagons	tons
Yate														
1961	1,196	5,276	107	1,132	156	1,801	165	792	543	2,025	285	2,727		
1962	1,204	6,656	146	1,390	171	2,164	88	669	520	2,122	223	2,648	56	177
1963	927	3,208	70	741	330	4,141	96	747	360	1,992	214	2,225	60	274
1964	1,041	4,213	1	16	379	4,873	1,175	171						
1965	794	7,696	247	3,233	266	3,473	103	1,336	194	1,965			78	864
Tytherington														
1960	6	26	349	5,834	79	990	1	1			34	409	1,589	26,362
1961	5	21	482	10,018	27	352					84	938	1,369	24,540
1962	1	1	412	8,442	53	638							798	15,482
1963	4	5	378	7,596	31	381							779	14,419
1964													1,226	22,371
1965	1	2	259	5,148									2,809	52,677
1966	1	1	341	7,080							8	164	959	18,209
Thornbury														
1960	115	363	66	558	364	4,284	3	3	20	29	8	48		
1961	892	5,697	27	191	372	4,459	5	12	10	43	8	48	3	20
1962	2,066	30,673	78	778	374	4,488	9	46	8	38	2	8		
1963	1,117	18,255	57	579	426	5,279	4	36	40	146			1	20
1964	901	12,012			404	5,162	17	21	56	567	1	13	15	17
1965					247	3,233								
Iron Acton														
1961					189	2,216								
1962					174	2,166	3	3						

Note: * Free-hauled i.e. for railway use.

Acknowledgements

I would like to thank N. Carter, R. Davis, G. Dixon, A. Gentle, W. Grainger, W. Hurcombe, D. Irwin, R. Jacob, D. Jenkins, W. Jones, C. Minnet, I. Pett, S.P.A. Savery, T. Slipp, C. Smith and C. Wake. Especial thanks are due to Colin Roberts for supplying information and checking the text and also to Peter Smith for the use of his station plans and drawings.

Bibliography

Books

Tytherington in the Past by Allan Baddeley (Author, 1994)
Bradshaw's Railway Manual (various years)
Bradshaw's Railway Guide (various years)
Industrial Archaeology of the Bristol Region by A. Buchanan & N. Cossons (David & Charles, 1969)
Clinker's Register of Closed Passenger Stations & Goods Depots by C.R. Clinker (Avon-Anglia, 1988)
Track Layout Diagrams of the GWR and BR/WR Section 20: South Gloucestershire by R.A. Cooke (Author, 1988)
The Midland Railway, A Chronology by J.V. Gough (RCTS, 1989)
LMS Engine Sheds Vol. 2 by C. Hawkins & G. Reeve (Wild Swan Publications, 1981)
Index to Local & Personal Acts (HMSO, 1949)
Industrial Locomotives of South Western England (Industrial Railway Society, 1977)
Biographical Dictionary of Railway Engineers by J. Marshall (David & Charles, 1978)
Midland Railway System Maps: Vol. 4 The Distance Diagrams (Peter Kay, no date)
Midland Railway System Maps: Vol. 6 The Gradient Diagrams (Peter Kay, 1999)
Railway Track Diagrams No. 3 Great Western (Quail Map, 2000)
An Historical Survey of the Midland in Gloucestershire by P. Smith (OPC, 1985)
Victoria County History: Gloucestershire (Oxford University Press)

Magazines and Newspapers

Bath & Cheltenham Gazette
Bath Chronicle
Bristol Times & Mirror
Bristol Mercury
Bristol Observer
Railway Magazine
Railway Observer

Index

Figures in **BOLD** indicate illustrations

Ambulance train, 87, 89
ARC/Hanson, 49, 67 *et seq.*, 91, 113 *et seq.*, 139
Bristol & Gloucester Railway, 5
Bristol & South Wales Union Railway, 10
Brunel, 13
Bus, 10, 85
Crossley, J.S., 5, 7 *et seq.*
Eckersley & Bayliss, 5, 7, 8
Fares, 10 *et seq.*
Frampton Cotterell, 5 *et seq.*, 37, 44, 93
Gradients, 7, 9, 37, 43, 49, 57, **64**, 69, 95, **99**, 133, 139
Grovesend, 7 *et seq.*, 87, 103, **106**, **108**, 109, **111**, 113, **114**, 125, 129, 131
Hardwicke, H.L., 49, 85, 105, 107, 109
Hutchinson, Lt-Col C.S., 8 *et seq.*
Iron Acton, 5, 7 *et seq.*, 37, 42 *et seq.*, 69, **70**, **73**, **78**, **80**, 85, **88**, 93, 101, 103, **112**, 129, 131, 133, **135**, 139, 142
Latteridge, 8, 43, ***47 et seq.***, **74**, **77**, 93, **110**, 131, **132**, 133, 139
Locomotives,
diesel,
39, 67, 69, 72, **75**, ***77 et seq.***, 91, **92**, **112**, **116**, 117, **118**, 128, 137
steam,
BR, **15**, **23**, ***28 et seq.***, **39**, ***44 et seq.***, **51**, ***53 et seq.***, **61**, ***63 et seq.***, **88**, **90**, **102**, ***110 et seq.***, 119, ***122 et seq.***, **125**, 126, **127**, 128, 132, 137
GWR, **27**, 119, 121
LMS, 85, 87, 89, 119, **120**, 121, 126
LNER, 87, 89, 126
MR, **20**, **22**, **82**, 119, 125
SR, 121, 127
Mangotsfield, 5, 137
McDonald, J.A., 7
Midland Railway, 5, 7, 13, 97, 101, 105, 107, 109
Permanent way, 8 *et seq.*, 133, 137, 139
Robertson, S., 8, 13
Savery, S., 67, 69, 75
Station staff, 11, 21, ***26 et seq.***, 43, 49, 57, **61**, **102**, 139
Thornbury, 5 *et seq.*, 57, ***58 et seq.***, 65, 67, 81, ***82 et seq.***, 85, 87, **88**, 89, **90**, 93 *et seq.*, 98, **99**, **102**, 103, 105, ***122 et seq.***, 125 *et seq.*, **127**, 129, **130**, 133, 139, 141 *et seq.*
Timetable, 11, 66, 81 *et seq.*, 92, 94, 96, 103 *et seq.*
Tunnels, 7, 9, 49, ***54 et seq.***, 56, 69, 85, **111**, 114, 128, 133, 139
Tytherington, 7 *et seq.*, 21, 28, 49, ***50 et seq.***, 67, **68**, ***70 et seq.***, 75, ***76 et seq.***, **79**, 85, 91, 94, 101, 103, 105, 107, **108**, 113, **114**, **116**, 117, 128, 130 *et seq.*, ***134 et seq.***, 138 *et seq.*, 142
Westerleigh, **12**, 13, 95, 126
Wickwar, 5
Yate, 5, 7, 9, **12**, 13, ***14 et seq.***, 21, ***22 et seq.***, 33, ***34 et seq.***, 37, ***38 et seq.***, **72**, 95,